Can Mainline Denominations Make a Comeback?

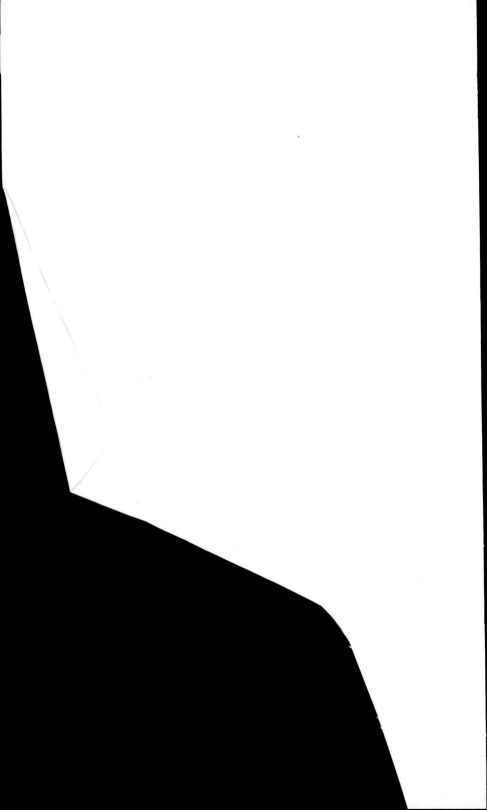

Can Mainline Denominations Make a Comeback?

Tony Campolo

Judson Press ® Valley Forge

Can Mainline Denominations Make a Comeback?
© 1995
Judson Press, Valley Forge, PA 19482-0851

Library of Congress Cataloging-in-Publication Data
Campolo, Anthony
   Can mainline denominations make a comeback? / Tony Campolo
     p. cm.
   Includes bibliographical references.
   ISBN 0-8170-1234-6 (pbk. : alk. paper)
   1. Protestant churches—United States. 2. Church renewal. 3. Liberalism (Religion)—United States—History—20th century. 4. Liberalism (Religion)—Protestant churches—History—20th century.
5. United States—Church history—20th century.
   I. Title.
   BR526.C348 1995
   262'.001'7097304—dc20   95-18064

Printed in the U.S.A.
95 96 97 98 99 00 01 02 8 7 6 5 4 3 2 1

Dedicated to
Roberta Hestenes
President of Eastern College,
whose support and encouragement help make
all that I do possible

Contents

Introduction

After more than three decades of decline, mainline denominations may face their first solid chance for recovery. The reasons are intriguing to say the least.

During the fifties and sixties, mainline denominations got into politics hot and heavy. Harvey Cox, in his classic book *The Secular City*, went so far as to suggest that we no longer consider God as Father. Instead, said Cox, we should consider God as the ultimate politician.

Mainline denominations were into heady stuff. They were at war against racism, sexism, and militarism. They were out to lobby for legislation that would end the war in Vietnam, stop racial discrimination, and abolish poverty. They called upon their preachers to declare the coming kingdom of God in sociological categories—and they did. Mainline denominations preached these things with such effectiveness that people got the message that these concerns were what the church was all about.

The problem was that many in these congregations needed a church that addressed other needs. Some had marriages that were falling apart; others had kids who were spaced out on drugs; and many who sat in the pews of mainline churches had lives that were, as the saying goes, "lived out in quiet desperation."

The socially conscious sermons that churchgoers with such deep personal needs were hearing from Sunday to Sunday left them hungry for something more. It wasn't long before they went looking elsewhere for that something more. And they found that elsewhere in nondenominational evangelical churches that were growing up all over the country. These people said they were looking for churches that preached the gospel. Specifically, they said they needed a gospel that would "save their souls" and the souls of their families.

The mainline churches that were being deserted had been so into social issues that they had forgotten there was another side to religion. They had forgotten that people need spiritual ecstasy, a sense of communion with God, a feeling of being caught up in the hands of One who could sustain them in trouble and direct them in times of confusion. That is what people looked for and found in the conservative, evangelical, nondenominational churches they joined.

But that was back in the fifties and sixties. Things have changed. Today those same conservative, evangelical, nondenominational churches that picked up the dropouts of politicized mainline churches have themselves gotten turned on to politics. Nowadays, fundamentalist churches, which once warned Christians against getting involved in politics, are tasting the elixir of power that makes drunkards of all who drink of it. Professional politicians have not been oblivious to this change, and it has not taken them long to get into nurturing the pastors of these growing nondenominational evangelical churches, knowing that in them they had ideological partners who could do much to deliver entire religious voting blocs into their camp.

There was no seduction in all of this. There was agreement. The preachers and the politicians agreed on just about everything. Laws on abortion and homosexuality, which had been progressively liberalized under the Democrats who had dominated Washington for decades, could now be challenged and changed. The feminist agenda, most symbolically represented by the Equal Rights Amendment, could be rolled back, and any real or imagined threat to the American family could be averted. It was all within the realm of the possible.

The Moral Majority, largely the creation of fundamentalist leader Jerry Falwell, had helped get the occupants of the White House elected and had every reason to expect that the new administration would be beholden to them. More needed to be done, of course, but the Religious Right was on its way. Moral Majority members believed that if they could just get more evangelical preachers across America to get *more* committed to the cause, they could turn the country around and reaffirm those old values that had gotten lost along the way. They were convinced that America had once been a Christian nation and were sure that if they just worked at it harder, they could make it a Christian nation again. The people in these new conservative, evangelical, nondenominational churches did not notice it at first, but little by little the old-time gospel was being replaced by the politics of the Religious Right.

Now, wouldn't it be ironic if people began to leave conservative, evangelical, nondenominational churches for exactly the same reason that they had left their mainline churches—if they decided that their evangelical churches were too much into politics and not enough into talking about Jesus? In many instances, that is just what is happening. The politics of the conservative, evangelical, nondenominational churches are increasingly identified with the politics of conservative Republicanism. This, of course, is in contrast with the politics of the mainline churches of the sixties, which espoused the liberal politics of the Democratic party. In either case, the result is that, at times, people feel like making the same request that a group of inquiring souls once asked Christ's disciples by the edge of a faraway sea: "Sir! We would see Jesus!"

What is even more interesting is that, while evangelical churches are becoming increasingly politicized, the mainline churches seem to be recovering some balance. Of course there will always be extremists who do strange things and keep alive the increasingly false impression that denominational preachers don't preach the gospel. But, in reality, increasing numbers of mainline preachers *have* recovered an emphasis on personal salvation in their sermons. They have done this while at the same time holding on to their established themes of biblical justice. Not only are they getting back to an emphasis on personal evangelism, but they are also rediscovering the power of the Bible. More and more they are communicating their call for social justice in scriptural terms. This biblically based balance gives them a holistic gospel to preach, and it is a gospel that, for a variety of reasons, is functionally fit for these times in which we live. With this balanced gospel message, mainline denominational preachers may have hit on that which will once again give them an impetus for growth.

But there are problems!

Just at the time when things might be looking up for mainline denominations, they find themselves being challenged to deal with the two most emotionally charged issues of our time—abortion and homosexuality. There are forces at work in each of the mainline denominations that would compel them to take definite stands on these issues. But a stand on either side of either one of these explosive issues would be sure to result in damaging losses of individuals and of entire churches for any mainline denomination.

This book is about how mainline denominations might handle such controversial issues so as to keep them from destroying the possibilities for renewal and recovery. I also try to outline other major problems that these denominations must solve if they are to regain some momentum for growth. I endeavor to summarize what went wrong that caused the decline in these denominations and why so many people who once were members of mainline churches have left them to join conservative, independent, nondenominational churches.

The American Baptist Churches in the U.S.A., a denomination that earlier went by the name "The American Baptist Convention" and before that by the name "The Northern Baptist Convention," is highly involved in all of these events and struggles and, as such, makes an ideal case study that can give us some idea of what is going on in other denominations. What is more important, the way this denomination of 1.5 million members handles the problems and the possibilities it now faces could easily provide the lessons that others will have to learn if their churches are going to make a comeback.

I myself am an American Baptist, and as part of this mainline denomination, I have witnessed its triumphs and difficulties. More importantly, I have had the opportunity to be involved in discussions with American Baptist pastors, laypersons, and denominational leaders about what can be done to revive this denomination and redefine its mission for the twenty-first century.

Consequently, this was an easy book to write, not because it needed little thought and effort, but because I have been thinking about the subject for years and have talked the subject matter over with countless persons who are as concerned about the future of the American Baptist Churches as I am.

From one end of this country to the other, there are people who love the American Baptist denomination and for a variety of reasons want to see it become healthy again. The most commonly cited reason for wanting American Baptist Churches to live long and prosper is the conviction that this denomination has a unique mission to play in American Christianity. There is a consensus among its thoughtful supporters that if that special mission can be discerned and articulated by its leaders, and if these leaders can inspire the members in local churches to become committed to it, a new era of dynamism (and maybe even growth) could begin.

While this book uses the American Baptist Churches, U.S.A. as a case study, the concerns, issues, and proposals that are the subject matter of this book have been paralleled in most other mainline denominations. The kind of soul searching, self-examination, and self-doubt that have been evident among American Baptists also have been evident among Methodists, Presbyterians, and people in other mainline churches. Those who love these historic denominations have been scrambling to find ways to reverse the trend of declining membership in their churches, even as they have been trying to figure out what God is calling them to be and to do in the years that lie ahead.

This is not a scholarly book. Instead, it is a set of reflections made by a sociologist who is also a preacher. My experiences as a preacher have taken me to places and enabled me to talk to people all across America and even abroad. These experiences have provided me with material that I have tried to interpret in sociological categories that will shed some light on the question of whether or not mainline denominations in general, and the American Baptist Churches in particular, can make a comeback. Just as important, I will try to answer another simple question that I am regularly asked: What has to change within our denomination in order to revitalize it and renew its growth?

There are two major divisions in this book. Part one provides an overview of what has happened to mainline denominations over the past half century. Special attention is given to the difficulties they have had as they have struggled with the controversial theological trends and the difficult social issues of the time. Any understanding of what must be done to rescue mainline churches from their present malaise will require that we know something of the social conditions and cultural forces that have forced them into their present difficult straits.

The first section of the book contains some suggestions for how mainline churches might respond to the unique challenges posed by emerging values and ideologies that have arisen in our culture. We will examine, in a limited way, how the advent of television has forced us to rethink both the content of the gospel and the ways in which we try to communicate its good news to this generation. We will try to probe the way in which an exaggerated self-centeredness, nurtured by what some have called "the culture of narcissism," has made it increasingly difficult to teach the cost of Christian discipleship. And we will give some attention to how the so-called culture wars have created within mainline denominations tensions that have threatened their survival.

The second part of this book provides seven suggestions that mainline churches might consider as they look for ways to regain their momentum for growth and social relevancy.

With the American Baptist Churches, U.S.A. as a case study, specific proposals will be made that other denominations may find applicable.

Authors always give some words of thanks when introducing a book. Specifically they thank those who provided them with some assistance in typing, proofreading, and editing. In this case those who assisted me did much more for me than any author has the right to expect from anyone:

I appreciate the able assistance of Mary Mugridge Nicol, my editor at Judson Press.

My wife, Peggy, and my son, Bart, spent long hours helping me to rewrite the manuscript for this book in order to make it readable.

My friend, Beverly Clark Carlson, gave me her valuable time to do research and provided necessary critiquing for the development of my ideas.

And most important, my associate, Susan Cole Dahlstrom, sacrificially gave herself in proofreading and typing the manuscript for this book. There is no way this book would be in your hands without her invaluable contributions.

Lastly, I want to say a thank-you to Jitsuo Morikawa. This onetime director of the Department of Evangelism for American Baptist Churches exercised a formative influence on my theological and social thinking, as he did on countless others. His theology and vision for the church's mission in the world forced me to rethink the categories of faith and practice that had, in my case, almost calcified. He did not so much provide answers to my questions as raise a host of new questions that I had never before considered.

If he were alive today, Jitsuo Morikawa might still consider me a fundamentalist, which in some ways I am. But I hope he would find me to be a grateful fundamentalist. He was a major influence responsible for driving me toward what theologians now call a " holistic doctrine of salvation." Evangelism, for me, is no longer simply a means of getting people ready for life in another world. Instead, it is a declaration of what God is doing in this world, both in the transforming of personal lives and in the transforming of the social order. In many respects this book reflects the holistic gospel that he communicated so well and that I am still trying to understand. I am grateful to Jitsuo Morikawa for helping me along this path of development.

Part I

Diagnosis

Chapter 1

Where Have All the Young Kids Gone?

In my attempt to deal with what has gone wrong with mainline denominations in general and with my own denomination, the American Baptist Churches, in particular, allow me to share with you three life stories.

The first is the story of a young man I once knew. He lived in the neighborhood in which I grew up. He was somewhat younger but, nevertheless, was a good friend. He is someone who was once part of a mainline denominational church but through the years drifted away, not only from the church of his boyhood, but from Christianity itself.

The second story is my own. I grew up in an American Baptist church and through the years have remained within my denomination. For me, church life in mainline Christendom worked out well. I had a good experience in the church of my childhood. The people of that church nurtured me well in the meaning of Christian discipleship. Since a good part of this book will be about my personal reflections on mainline denominational Christianity, it would be good for you to know just where I started and why I have a vested interest in seeing to it that mainline denominations survive.

Third, I will tell you about my son's experience with churches. We started him off in a mainline church, but it failed to turn him on to vital Christianity. In many respects, the failure of that church demonstrates much of why mainline denominationalism is failing. The good news is that my son eventually did come into a strong commitment to Christ, but that was because of his joining a highly evangelical "superchurch" that grew up in our neighborhood. In many ways, what made that church such an effective means for bringing my son into a personal commitment to Christ illustrates what it is about nondenominational evangelical churches that have enabled them to grow and prosper during the last twenty-five years, even while mainline churches have been in decline.

The Story of Jack Lawson

Nothing like my son's experience ever happened to Jack Lawson. During his years of growing up, he attended a mainline denominational church. He was Methodist because the Lawson family had always been Methodist. And his family took him to church every Sunday because the Lawson family had always gone to church on Sundays.

When Jack started college, he stopped going to church, not because he was against it or had stopped believing in God. It wasn't anything like that. He gave up going to church simply because he found it boring.

Jack was a baby boomer—a member of the first generation ever socialized on television. The mediocre preaching and mundane music of his home church were unable to hold the attention of a kid who had been raised on "the tube." Television altered the ways in which people communicated, and the lecture method of Jack's hometown preacher was no match for a media that featured big-time stars, dazzling technical effects, and high adventure. Sunday school was not as interesting as *Howdy Doody*, and the Sunday sermon was a far cry from *Mission Impossible*. Jack gave up on church—not out of a sense of rebellion, but simply because he lost interest.

His minister, the Reverend Peter Downs, worried about losing the likes of Jack. It seemed to him as though the brightest and best of those who had grown up in his church were drifting away from "the household of God." He tried what many ministers tried during the turbulent sixties. He tried to be *relevant*. The message that Pastor Downs and his fellow pastors heard from the seminaries was that unless they preached relevantly about the issues of the day, the younger generation would leave the church. "This generation," Pastor Downs was told, "is socially concerned. And unless the youth of this generation hear sermons on the 'tough issues' of the day, they will write off the church, and with it they will write off the gospel." Denominational leaders gave the same warning.

At a pastor's conference, Pastor Downs had heard someone quote the stirring words of the German-Swiss theologian Karl Barth: "Each day you should read the Bible in one hand while reading the newspaper in the other." And Pastor Downs tried to do just that! He preached sermons condemning racism and the war in Vietnam. He talked about the need to pay "reparations" to the blacks of America as one way to repent of the ways in which they had been economically exploited by the white establishment. And he explained how his denomination was designing programs that would help to bring about some kind of racial and economic equality.

He tried! Pastor Downs really tried! And overall he made a good impression on Jack. As a matter of fact, contrary to Bob Dylan's warning, Jack felt that Pastor Downs had a lot of good ideas, in spite of the fact that he was over thirty. But in the end, all his pastor's efforts didn't do what had to be done to hold Jack in the fellowship of the church. As relevant as Pastor Downs tried to be, he failed to win the allegiance of this bright and "with it" young man. Even if Pastor Downs seemed all right to him, Jack found the overall effect of what went on during the eleven o'clock hour deadly. And so, he did not so much reject Reverend Downs' message or his own belief in the existence of God; it was simply that he bade the whole ecclesiastical scene a fond farewell!

My Own Story

The church fared better with some of us than it did with Jack. It certainly did with me. I also grew up in a mainline denominational church. My boyhood church was a member of the American Baptist Convention.[1] I don't remember much about our Sunday services. I have a sense that the sermons were somewhat less "relevant" than those of Pastor Downs. I liked the choir because my sisters were in it and I liked my sisters. But what really kept me in the New Berean Baptist Church in West Philadelphia was the fellowship.

The word "fellowship" really meant something to me in my growing-up years. I have been to many churches since, I have never been able to find a group of church people who were such good friends. The folks at New Berean made sure that kids like me had fun. We had a tiny "band box" gym, but we put it to good use. We had a church basketball team, and to play on the team I had to regularly attend the Sunday night youth group meeting. I loved basketball, I loved the youth group, and I loved New Berean.

Our church made sure that the boys and girls in the youth group got to go to Camp Unami during the summer months, and my camping experiences had a profound effect on me. Whatever might be said about the shortcomings of denominational programming, it would be hard to fault the camping programs. If a statistical study were to be made among American Baptists as to where they had made serious commitments to serve Christ, I think that half of them would say that it was at camps like Camp Unami.

I am not quite sure what made those camps work. The staffs were less than professional. The facilities were slightly better than adequate. The food and the "bug juice" they served in the mess halls were terrible. And yet, at those Saturday night campfire services—on the fiftieth verse of

"Kum Ba Ya"—something special would always happen. I can still hear the camp director giving the talk that has been heard a thousand times at a thousand other campfire meetings:

> Kids, it's easy to be a Christian when you're up here on the mountaintop surrounded by other Christians. But will you be able to live for Christ when you leave here and go down to the valley? when you're back home with the crowd at school, with the kids in the neighborhood, with the gang you run with? Will you be able to live for Jesus then?

For this youngster, those words were a challenge straight from God, and I said yes. Tears rolled down my cheeks as the other campers and I formed a "fellowship circle" around the campfire and, holding hands, we sang:

> "Lord, we are able." Our spirits are Thine.
> Remold them, make us, Like Thee, divine.
> Thy guiding radiance Above us shall be
> A beacon to God, To love and loyalty.[2]

Every summer I went through the same ritual; and every summer, as corny as sophisticates might deem it to be, it always worked. And over the years my commitment grew, not only for Christ, but for the church that sent me to Camp Unami.

But mine was the generation before Jack Lawson's. This was in the late 1940s—before TV. It was a time of innocence, when people still believed in the American Dream and in the goodness of our government. It was before Gary Powers and his ill-fated U-2 flight—before the onslaught of disillusionment. It was a gentler and simpler time when church was what most Americans were into, and our other social institutions seemed to be working just fine.

My own religion was experiential. I was into being "born again" and having a personal relationship with Jesus. And even if church worship wasn't all that exciting for me, knowing Jesus was. Actually, I couldn't quite figure out why church wasn't exciting. After all, we could shout and scream at football games, so why weren't we shouting and screaming at church? Wasn't Jesus more exciting than football? Evidently he wasn't, at least not at eleven o'clock on Sunday morning at the New Berean Baptist Church.

Bart's Story

My son became a Christian in a nondenominational church. I had come to suburban Philadelphia to teach at Eastern College, and our family looked for a church in our neighborhood. We had given a nearby American Baptist church a try, but our children didn't like it, so eventually the family settled into a United Methodist church where a number of their schoolmates attended.

It was the early 1970s, and for mainline denominations the glory era of the fifties—when traditional Protestant churches had record turnouts—was fading. Almost forgotten were those days when mainline denominations had been endowed with a self-assurance that bordered on arrogance. Times had changed. The old formulas for getting people into the churches weren't working anymore. Such was the case for this United Methodist church. It had a lot of good people in it and a more than adequate pastor. But it was stagnant: not much growth, very little dynamism.

Out on the West Coast, some professors at Fuller Theological Seminary were trying to scientifically isolate those factors that would make growth happen in a church like this one, but they were not yet being taken very seriously by leaders of major denominations. For the most part, churches were simply trying to use the means and methods they had always used, hoping those techniques would work if they were employed with more diligence.

All the mainline churches in our neighborhood were like this. The loss of interest in church was marked by these churches cutting out any "extra" services. They all had given up Sunday evening services and midweek prayer meetings. I can remember my mother saying:

> Those who come on Sunday morning
>   love the preacher.
> Those who come on Sunday evening
>   love the church.
> Those who come on Wednesday evening
>   love the Lord.

In the fifties, we made judgments about churches that did not have Sunday evening services. We thought of them as liberal or modernistic. We were convinced that any church with a zeal for the Lord and a concern for the lost would have its doors open so that people could hear the gospel on Sunday evenings. But that was a long time ago. With television becoming a nightly ritual and the breakdown of the special-ness that had once marked Sundays, the crowds for evening services evaporated, and following that, the services were canceled.

Midweek prayer meetings also passed from the scene, but in their place small groups became popular in many churches. Church of the Saviour in Washington, D.C., set the pace for small-group ministries by demonstrating that in small groups people could experience with each other a special spiritual intimacy that might be something like that known in the early church. Words like *koinonia* became part of the common vocabulary of those who traveled in mainline denominational circles. And indeed, to those who strategized for established churches, small-group ministries seemed to be one of the few innovations that had good results.

The idea of meeting in small groups on various nights throughout the week to study and discuss some religious theme or book or to do Bible study was promoted and accepted far and wide. But these small groups appealed mostly to *young married couples* who were seeking a deeper walk in the Christian faith. And as good as they were for holding on to those young adults who took Christianity seriously, these small groups did not seem to have the same attraction for those who were outside the domain of the church. Something more was needed if a new generation were going to be reached with the gospel.

My son found that "something more" at a new church that was created in our neighborhood. Just as Bart was coming into his teenage years, some highly evangelical Christians established a new congregation that rapidly grew into the most dynamic church in the area.

There were various reasons why that church picked up new members, but for many the thing that made the church attractive was that it had a vital and well-planned youth program. Bart loved being a part of the youth group, and it was through the ministry of its leaders that he came into an intensive and lasting relationship with Christ.

That church in general, and the youth group in particular, had been patterned after the Willow Creek Community Church in South Barrington, Illinois. The staff at Willow Creek Church were experts in marketing, and they had done thorough research to determine what kind of church program would "sell" to the generation of Boomers, who were the target group for their ministry. One of the essential parts of their marketing research was the discovery of a need for professionally run youth programs. For a church to grow, it had to be sure to attract junior and senior high young people. It had to be entertaining and exciting in ways that appealed to a generation reared on the high-energy qualities of TV. The Willow Creek church had figured out how to do that, and the new church in our neighborhood copied that model down to the last detail.

The youth group to which my son belonged was state-of-the-art stuff. The leaders of the program carefully planned each meeting to include contemporary music, drama, short but highly effective explanations of the gospel, and a lot of fun. The programs were polished and rehearsed. Compared to the amateurish youth programs of most traditional churches, they were nothing short of sensational.

The youth group meetings, which drew more than three hundred kids, were just the beginning of the church's plan to evangelize the young people of the community. They had a full-time youth pastor who spent long hours reaching teen-agers like my son in a personal, one-on-one fashion. He arranged breakfast meetings during which he could talk over spiritual matters with them face-to-face. And he was able to get young people to witness to their friends. It was through such a witnessing friend that Bart made his decision to give his life to Christ and become involved in Christian ministry. There was much more to this church than just the youth program. The church abandoned traditional worship forms. Sunday morning services were designated for "seekers" rather than for believers. They were planned to appeal to those who had drifted away from the church or had never been part of it at all. The computer expression "user-friendly" was applied to these Sunday services because they were structured to be nonthreatening to those who were not in the habit of attending regular church worship. There was no pressure on people to join. The Sunday morning service didn't even include an offering. The service was an entertaining gift to the visitors. It was designed to make them feel at home, and it did just that.

It wasn't long before this church had drawn in large numbers of the unchurched in the community. The neighbor-hood was abuzz over the success and growth of the new church. It wasn't long before members from the neighboring mainline churches began leaving their home congregations to become a part of this new user-friendly congregation.

It would be an easy thing for sophisticated critics to write off in cavalier fashion such user-friendly churches by calling them compromises with the prevailing culture. But such judgments are unfair. While their Sunday services might seem superficial to the casual observer, the churches that followed the Willow Creek model more than compensated for that appearance of superficiality. Most had a second service sometime during the week at which the committed members came together for intensive Bible study, prayer, and worship. Beyond that, these churches established networks of small groups that met in private homes throughout their respective communities. The fact was that these superchurches, many of which drew two thousand or more people to their Sunday morning programs, provided more intimate fellowship, offered more intensive Bible study, and created more of a sense of belonging than did most of the mainline congregations that were a fraction of their size.

Superchurches have an advantage over congregations of smaller size because they are able to employ multiple-member staffs. A superchurch can have full-time specialists in youth work, children's ministry, marital counseling, pastoral care, missions, music, small-group ministry, worship, evangelism, and church administration. The church that my son joined even had a minister for the children of divorced parents, of whom there were many in our neighborhood.

To misuse a Bible passage, when it comes to superchurches versus moderate-sized denominational churches, it can be said, "To those who have shall be given; and from those who have not shall be taken away even that which they have." Superchurches can have multiple-member staffs because they have growing congregations, and they have growing congregations because they have multiple-member staffs. Smaller denominational churches that lack the resources to compete lose members left and right to these superchurches.

When all the pros and cons of these new highly evangelical churches are argued, the fact remains that they are functionally fit for the requisites of a new generation that has found traditional church life uninteresting and unrelated to life as they are living it. So far as I am concerned, I am glad for churches like this one. Who knows what would have happened to my son if no such church had been born in our town?

Chapter 2

They Were the Best of Times and the Worst of Times

To trace what has happened to mainline denominations during the last three decades, I want to tell you more of what happened to me during those years as a member of the American Baptist Convention. In many ways, what went on in the ABC during those years demonstrates both the good and bad about the response of mainline denominations to the crises of the times and the forces of social change that were then at work in society.

Mainline denominations like the ABC have struggled to make their churches relevant to societal needs. Nobody is about to question that. They may have failed to develop the kinds of programs that "turn on" young people and bring in new members, but there can be no doubt that they have tried to address the pressing issues of the day. As society struggled with the moral ambiguities of the Vietnam War, the challenges of the civil rights movement, and the disturbing insights of feminist thinking, the leaders of mainline denominations tried hard to have their people address these concerns. Out of the context of biblical reflections, they endeavored to set forth prophetic responses to these controversial developments. What they said about such things in the resolutions they passed at their conventions, conferences, and general assemblies was often courageous, but just as often alienating. These denominational leaders made a lot of people mad, and they were responsible for the loss of a great deal of popular support.

But perhaps even more detrimental to the well-being of mainline denominations was the fact that they focused on social concerns to such an extent that the pastoral concerns of their churches were neglected. Churches not only needed to mobilize their members to participate in the struggle for societal justice; it was also necessary for them to evangelize and minister to the personal needs of their people. Mainline churches, while struggling to do the former, often failed to address the latter concerns. Consequently, they became less and less effective at holding on to members and recruiting new ones.

Within the American Baptist Churches these tendencies were particularly evident. In the fifties and sixties, the denominational executive chosen to lead the churches in the field of evangelism did little to inspire churches to win converts and build sensitive, nurturing ministries. Jitsuo Morikawa, perhaps the most dynamic and brilliant leader that American Baptists have had in the past fifty years, took over the Department of Evangelism and proceeded to redefine what evangelism was all about. Instead of defining evangelism as the simple declaration of how Christ's death removes sin and guarantees personal salvation, Morikawa gave it a wider meaning. He helped Baptists to understand that evangelism was the declaring of the Good News about all that God is doing in the world. Salvation, according to Morikawa, had to be understood in cosmic terms. Christ, through his own death and resurrection, set loose redemptive powers that would save not only individuals but the entire world. Political and economic structures were to be seen as within the scope of his saving work.

Armed with such a holistic doctrine of salvation, Morikawa became a voice for social change. Throughout the American Baptist Convention, there was serious reconsideration of what evangelism was all about. The God whom Morikawa preached was a God who was at work in the world, freeing oppressed people and lifting up the downtrodden. He sent out the word that the American Baptist Convention would be a denomination committed to rooting out racial discrimination and pursuing economic justice.

The denomination responded well to Morikawa's leadership. There were trials and tensions, but through it all, a new tone was set. In the midst of the agonies of the Vietnam era, there were resolutions calling for the support of peace. And in theological conferences there was talk of what it meant to evangelize social structures. Morikawa talked about delivering social structures from the demonic powers that made them destructive to the well-being of society. He called us to the task of proclaiming the good news that, through the church, God was bringing these social structures under the lordship of Christ. In the end, according to Morikawa, God's justice would reign in history. He called Christians to serve as agents of change in all sectors of the political-economic system to the end that God's will would be done on earth as it was in heaven.

The whole purpose of winning people to Christ changed. Instead of trying to preach a salvation that was aimed at ensuring people a blissful destiny in the next world, with Morikawa we were called to preach a message that would invite people to participate in God's transforming work in society.

God, it was argued, does not want to save us just to go to heaven when we die. God wants more for us than that. God wants to save and sanctify us so that we will do God's work in the midst of this present age.

Despite what his critics said, Morikawa's theology was grounded in the Bible. For many of us, his preaching and writing opened up the Scriptures in ways that made the salvation story brilliantly relevant to what was going on during the sixties and seventies. Evangelism, according to his biblical insights, now included the good news about what

God was doing to tear down the social barriers that keep people from fellowship with one another. It was a message of reconciliation for people alienated by war, and a call for Christians to make social justice a historical reality. Our task was to win people to Christ so that they would be recruited to such revolutionary tasks.

As our blood ran hot with the vision for the role of the church that was promoted by Morikawa, we made one serious mistake. We failed to pay enough attention to bringing new members into our churches. It was not that Morikawa put down the traditional idea of evangelism as a means for getting people saved and baptized into church membership. It was just that this particular emphasis was not given the prominence needed for dramatic church growth. Changing the world, not growing religious institutions, was the mission that dominated his understanding of what Christians were supposed to be about.

During 1964, when Morikawa was at the peak of his influence, Baptists worldwide entered into a year of evangelistic emphasis called the Baptist Jubilee Advance. To those in the Southern Baptist Convention, this translated into a call to plant a thousand new churches and a goal of adding a million new members to their membership rolls. For American Baptists, church growth and the winning of converts were less than overpowering concerns. There were some in the denominational hierarchy who ridiculed an evangelistic program that, as they said, "made us into head hunters and evaluated success in terms of how many scalps we could wear on our belts."

As a matter of fact, there actually was an alternative definition of the role of the church being articulated. It was called "remnant theology." This was a belief that the calling of the church is to be a faithful but small group of people who live out the values of the Kingdom of God and bear witness to the new humanity that God is calling into being. Adding members to the church was not our primary task. Rather it was to be a people who modeled to the world what God's kingdom would be like at the climax of history.

In the Hebrew Bible, when Israel failed to live out the love and justice prescribed for the people of God, there was, nevertheless, within Israel a faithful remnant, as described in Isaiah 10:21-22: "The remnant shall return, even the remnant of Jacob, unto the mighty God. For though thy people Israel be as the sand of the sea, yet a remnant of them shall return."

To this faithful remnant was given the historical responsibility to be a people in whom the will of God for all humanity would be demonstrated. In American Baptist circles there was a tendency to identify with this Old Testament remnant.

A commonly used illustration for this role of the church is given by Harvey Cox in his book *The Secular City*, where he refers to the city of Nowa Huta in Poland. After the Communists took over, they created this city to be a living demonstration of what was in store for all of Poland in the years that lay ahead. They provided the best in housing, schools, and public services. Only those who were ideologically pure Communists were allowed to live there. Nowa Huta was to be the perfect place to live. And the purpose of all of this was so that the Communist party could point to this city as the vision of what the world would be like when the Communists finally realized their aspirations for society.

Accordingly, the church was to be God's Nowa Huta. It was to be a people who modeled the coming kingdom of God. The people of the church were to so live out the will of God that the community they created would enable the rest of the world to see what God had in store for them at the end of history. It was to be a fellowship without racism, war, poverty, sexism, and environmental disasters. According to remnant theology, the church should be that remnant of humanity to which we can point and say, "See! That's the kind of society God is going to create for the entire human race." Such a church need not be a growing institution. It need only be a faithful remnant of radically committed Christians.

Unfortunately, this remnant theology became a self-fulfill-ing prophecy. I am not too sure how faithful American Baptist churches were to the biblical model, but by the 1980s they certainly were well on their way to becoming a remnant. Membership figures in annual reports bear this out. The American Baptist denomination was shrinking, and only the fact that many African-American churches became dually aligned with the denomination during this period kept the statistics from reading like an obituary column.

It is with a great deal of ambivalence that I reflect on those difficult decades during which Morikawa's influence held sway in the American Baptist Convention. On my own personal level, Morikawa opened up whole new vistas of Christian faith. For me, he made being an evangelist the most exciting and important calling imaginable. His vision gave my preaching a new cutting edge. Evangelism would never again be reduced simply to getting people to believe some propositional truths, the acceptance of which would guarantee them eternal life. The "otherworldly" nature of my messages was replaced with a declaration that salvation was also a "this world" message.

When I called people to come down the aisle during the "invitation," it was not just as a means of preparing them for the next life. I came to believe that what I really was doing was recruiting people to join in a movement, that becoming a Christian meant nothing less than surrendering to the lordship of Christ so that he might use us as agents of his revolution. The call to give one's life to Christ was transformed into a call to become instruments through which he could address the pressing concerns of this world.

"Saved" people were no longer talking about pie-in-the-sky-when-they-die. They were a people ordained to enter into every sector of society as agents of change. They were to be the leaven that would permeate the social order with a transforming presence that would work against racism, sexism, militarism, homophobia, and economic injustice.

In response to Morikawa's influence, many of us experienced a subtle shift in our preaching from declaring the theology of Paul to declaring the ethics of the kingdom of God as declared by Jesus, especially as they are laid out in the Sermon on the Mount. In my own preaching, I in no way de-emphasized the need to have a personal transforming relationship with the resurrected Christ. To the contrary, being personally converted was more important than ever. But the *purpose* of personal conversion had changed. The idea that conversion was designed to enable the individual to escape eternal punishment and get into heaven seemed to me to make the salvation process egoistic and selfish. I came to see that we were saved not to guarantee heaven for ourselves, but to serve the needs of others. God's Son was calling us, I believed, to be recruits for an army that would do battle with the principalities and powers of this world. I was convinced that people with a personal relationship with Christ were to be a people committed to alleviating suffering and to declaring the good news that God's kingdom was at hand.

Loving Jesus was, for me, no longer some abstract pietistic exercise to be carried out in detachment from the world. Rather, I came to understand it as a response to what Jesus said to his disciples in Matthew 25:

> When the Son of man shall come in his glory, and all the holy angels with him, then shall he sit upon the throne of his glory: And before him shall be gathered all nations: and he shall separate them one from another, as a shepherd divideth his sheep from the goats: And he shall set the sheep on his right hand, but the goats on the left. Then shall the King say unto them on his right hand, Come, ye blessed of my Father, inherit the kingdom prepared for you from the foundation of the world: For I was an hungred, and ye gave me meat: I was thirsty, and ye gave me drink: I was a stranger, and ye took me in: Naked, and ye clothed me: I was sick, and ye visited me: I was in prison, and ye came unto me. Then shall the righteous answer him, saying, Lord, when saw we thee an hungred, and fed thee? or thirsty, and gave thee drink? When saw we thee a

stranger, and took thee in? or naked, and clothed thee? Or
when saw we thee sick, or in prison, and came unto thee?
And the King shall answer and say unto them, Verily I say
unto you, Inasmuch as ye have done it unto one of the least
of these my brethren, ye have done it unto me. Then shall
he say also unto them on the left hand, Depart from me,
ye cursed, into everlasting fire, prepared for the devil and
his angels: For I was an hungred, and ye gave me no meat:
I was thirsty, and ye gave me no drink: I was a stranger,
and ye took me not in: naked, and ye clothed me not: sick,
and in prison, and ye visited me not. Then shall they also
answer him, saying, Lord, when saw we thee an hungred,
or athirst, or a stranger, or naked, or sick, or in prison, and
did not minster unto thee? Then shall he answer them,
saying, Verily I say unto you, Inasmuch as ye did it not to
one of the least of these, ye did it not to me. And these shall
go away into everlasting punishment: but the righteous
into life eternal (Matthew 25:31-46).

This passage of Scripture became central to my preaching.
There have been few sermons that I have preached over the
past quarter of a century in which these verses have not been
cited. My understanding of what Jesus said in these verses
is that he uses the poor and the oppressed whom I meet on
the streets of my city and who suffer in the barrios of Third
World countries to present himself to me. Whenever I look
into the eyes of those suffering from demonic social injustice,
I have this growing awareness that Jesus himself is staring
back at me. I feel him coming *through* them and presenting
himself to me, challenging me to his service. Strange as this
may sound, the thinking of Jitsuo Morikawa, a mainline
denominational executive, caused me to recast my beliefs
into the forms of Franciscan theology.

Those who have taken the time to learn about the life of
St. Francis of Assisi know of a special encounter he had with
a leper. One day when Francis was riding on his horse, his
way was blocked by a man who had leprosy. The man's face
and hands had been rotted by his dreaded disease. To Francis,

the man was a sickening sight. But, out of his compassion, he got down from his horse and went over to the leper, giving him his money and his cloak. Then as a parting gesture of love, he kissed the diseased man. Francis climbed back on his horse and turned to bid him good-bye. But the road was empty. The leper had literally disappeared! It was only then that Francis realized that the leper had been none other than Christ himself. From that day on, Francis regarded every poor, sick, or suffering person he met as though that person were Christ, because, as far as he was concerned, every such person *was* Christ.

For me, that event in the life of St. Francis has been repeated in less dramatic ways over and over again. I have come to believe that there is no better way to love Jesus than to love him in the lost or the last or the least. For having come to this way of loving Jesus, I again owe a great debt to Jitsuo Morikawa. He was the one who led me to connect mystical encounters with Christ to my encounters with people in need.

Once I made that connection, everything changed for me. Not only did I start responding to hurting people on a personal level by giving what I could and should to them, but on the societal level I grew increasingly impatient with those social and economic structures that were responsible for their sufferings. It didn't take long for me to link increasing commitments to activist movements for justice with my growing love for the Lord.

None of these changes in my thinking swayed me from my basic evangelical convictions. I still believed in the infallibility of Scripture and all the doctrines outlined in the Apostle's Creed. I was, in the eyes of most American Baptists, still a fundamentalist.

Unfortunately, those who thought like I did found themselves marginalized by the executive leadership of the American Baptist Convention. Like the leaders of most mainline denominations, they tended toward embracing theological beliefs that were more liberal than the rank-and-file memberships of their churches, and people like me still looked like dangerous fundamentalists to them. So while they applauded the ways in which we new-type evangelicals brought together an emphasis on a personal relationship with Christ and a passion to right the wrongs of society, they were, nevertheless, uneasy with us.

Our reliance on old-style evangelistic preaching and our constant references to the need for personal conversion may have seemed too much for those denominational leaders who had experienced much trouble from old-time fundamentalists. Our newfound social dimensions to the understanding of salvation did not dissuade us from the need to hold old-time revival meetings in which we called upon people to come to the altar to the singing of "Just As I Am." Little about our style had changed. What was different was the *context* of the decision-making process. It had previously been a call to accept Jesus as personal Savior; it was now much more. The decision-making process had been expanded to a call to surrender to the lordship of Christ and to follow his leading in the transformation of society.

Fundamentalism had split the denomination both in the thirties and in the forties, and the executive leadership of the American Baptist Convention may have feared that we were nothing more than up-to-date versions of the people who had led those schismatic movements. Like all mainline denominations, the ABC had been burned by the sectarian dimensions of fundamentalism, and its leaders cast a wary eye on any who might rekindle the intolerant absolutistic mind-set that had generated denominational civil wars. We certainly talked like fundamentalists. With our emphasis on the infallibility of Scripture and our rejection of modernistic theology, we must have come across as the same old wolves not too cleverly disguised in sheep's clothing.

What many American Baptist denominational leaders did not realize was that we were a whole new breed of theological conservatives who were not into denominational fratricide and schism. While we were strongly committed to what we considered to be a classical orthodox Christian theology, we were quite ready to accept as Christian brothers and sisters those who did not agree with us on doctrines we considered to be of secondary importance. All we asked was that Jesus Christ be acknowledged as Lord, Savior, and God. If that simple theological commitment (which, incidently, was the basic theological requirement for being a part of the National and World Council of Churches) could be adhered to, we were convinced we had a basis for Christian solidarity.

Back in the early seventies, I was invited to speak at a nationwide gathering of American Baptist youth. The meeting, called "The Great Gathering," was held at Green Lake, Wisconsin, our denominational assembly grounds. I was given the opportunity to deliver the keynote address on the opening night of this get-together. I did my usual thing and asked young people to come forward and give their lives to Christ. My message was a call to commitment that required those who responded to give themselves to God's mission of changing the world. There was a great deal of Morikawa's emphasis on societal reconstruction in what I said, but the style was an imitation of a Billy Graham evangelistic crusade.

The next morning a meeting was called by those running the assembly, and I was informed in no uncertain terms that there was no place for that kind of preaching at this gathering. Some accused me of playing on the emotions of young people. Others said that I had manipulated the crowd into making decisions that were little more than exercises in group psychology.

It didn't take much for me to figure out that on the national level there was little appreciation for a preacher like me in the American Baptist Convention at that time. I represented a kind of evangelism that many regarded as out of place in modern mainline denominational life.

All of that has changed now, but in the early sixties, negative attitudes toward mass evangelism were all too evident in the mainline denominations, even if that evangelism was balanced with a strong commitment to social action.

I don't want to create the impression that there was no place for me in American Baptist denominational life at that time. While I might not have had much acceptance on the national level, I had more than my share of opportunities for ministry on the state level.

The American Baptist Convention always has been a two-level organization. Back then, the denomination was made up of state conventions, each of which was incorporated as a somewhat independent entity. The leaders of state conventions tended to represent a theological posture that was more conservative than that of the national leadership. On the state level, executives were more in touch with those in the pews and more cognizant of what had to happen to build up local churches. State leaders were less into new theologies of evangelism and more into finding ways to build up local churches. Consequently, state executives were more than willing to utilize those evangelistic and church-growth techniques that guaranteed more members would be added to their rolls and more financial support would be available to undergird their ministries.

I don't want to convey the idea that cynical pragmatic motives drove these state-level officials. Quite to the contrary, these state-level leaders were committed to the more traditional approaches to the evangelistic mission of the church. Local congregations in states where there were large numbers of churches representing a more traditional mindset (such as in Ohio, West Virginia, Michigan, Indiana, and Pennsylvania) chose leaders who represented their beliefs. And their state leaders often were in tension with those in the national offices at Valley Forge. State conventions frequently had programs that reflected a more conservative and evangelistic style than one would expect after talking to national leaders. And many of us who could not gain wide acceptance on the national level found a ready welcome for our ministries on the state level. None of this compensated for the fact that on the national level something vital was being lost. Efforts on the state level could not change the reality that this denomination, while assuming a strong prophetic stance on social issues, was failing to give sufficient attention to what would grow churches.

Chapter 3

Mainline Churches and Cultural Lag

I

There are those who claim that mainline denominations are in decline because they are theologically liberal and don't preach the gospel. I don't believe that!

Admittedly, as I have pointed out, the leaders of mainline denominations often hold to beliefs that are far to the left of the overwhelming majority of the constituent members of their local congregations. Every sociologist who has studied religion in America knows that. But, by most standards established to measure evangelicalism, the preachers in the local churches of mainline denominations would easily score high marks. Sunday after Sunday, those who serve local congregations try their best to make the old-time gospel message clear and convincing. They talk about salvation by grace and through faith in Jesus. They preach the cross and the resurrection. They pray for their people, and they invite them to surrender their lives to the lordship of Christ. Most of them believe the Bible to be the infallible Word of God and give expression to values that would make most fundamentalists feel comfortable.

When the leaders of mainline denominations take liberal

stands on controversial issues, the pastors of most local churches are very likely to be upset. And when the World Council of Churches or the National Council of Churches seems to support revolutionary ideologies that sound to them more like Marx than Jesus, these same pastors are likely to be in the vanguard of protest.

While eschewing the label "fundamentalist," mainline denominational preachers are very likely to claim commitment to the essential doctrines of evangelical Christianity. The reasons that these preachers do not want to be identified with fundamentalism have little to do with theology and more to do with their rejection of the attitudes and legalism that they claim pervade the fundamentalistic subculture. Fundamentalism, they claim, is a subculture marked by authoritarianism and judgmental pieties. But it would be difficult to discern any unorthodox doctrines in the preaching of the basically conservative preachers in mainline churches. This was borne out in my own experiences.

One summer when I was in my late teens, I went to a Bible conference for a week. It was one of those conferences at which fundamentalist preachers ranted and raged against any denominations related to the National or World Council of Churches. I was assured that these organizations were fronts for the Communist party and that most of the pastors of denominational churches had been duped into accepting the party line. I was made to believe that my own pastor had been sucked into this mode of the Antichrist and that if I knew what was good for me, I would get out of that apostate denomination and go to a church where I could hear "The Word."

When that week of indoctrination with antidenominationalism was over, I returned home determined to confront what I believed were the demonic powers that had taken over the New Berean Baptist Church. I made an appointment to see my pastor right after the Sunday morning service. I was determined to challenge him to give up his American Baptist Convention links and get back to preaching the gospel instead of feeding us his liberal line. But as I sat there on that particular Sunday and listened to the sermon, I was close to amazed at what I heard. My pastor preached from the Bible! He made the way of salvation clear! Everything he said seemed right on target!

The more I thought about it and the longer I reflected, the more I realized that he had always preached like that. He may have lacked some charisma, and the overall impact of our Sunday services could have been more evangelistic in tone, but in retrospect, there was no denying the fact that my American Baptist Convention pastor preached the gospel and that my church was very much in the business of trying to win people to Christ. He may not have done it very well, but that's what he tried to do.

What I realized was true about my church back then can be said today about the majority of churches in most mainline denominations. Those churches may seem to be weighed down with deadly rituals and traditions, but in the midst of it all, there is often a heartfelt desire "to tell the old, old story of Jesus and his love." For the most part, the folks in mainline church pews still want to hear what the Bible says. Furthermore, they are so convinced that the Bible is a revelation from God that, if the Bible says something, they believe it to be absolute infallible truth.

If you want to figure out what's wrong with mainline denominational churches, you will have to look for the trouble somewhere else. Whatever is wrong with mainline denominational churches, the problem does not lie with what the preachers preach or what the church people believe. Strange as it may seem to their critics, the broad base of members and most of the preachers in mainline churches are sound believers and proclaimers of a solid, historically tested gospel message. The reasons for the failure of mainline churches to grow in the face of the growth of the new nondenominational superchurches and, in the case of American Baptists, in contrast to the growth of its sister denomination, the Southern Baptist Convention, lie elsewhere.

II

From the perspective of a sociologically aware expert in marketing, it could be said that our churches just are not programmatically structured to meet and relate to the kind of people whose consciousness and needs have been molded by social forces that have been playing themselves out since the beginning of the 1960s. In particular, there are three of these forces that have overtaken traditional Christianity and made mainline churches into victims of cultural lag. These three forces are television, the emergence of the culture of narcissism, and the advent of the culture wars.

If mainline churches are going to make a comeback over the next couple of decades, they must come to grips with each of these social forces. It will not do to preach against them in the hope that people will disengage from them and embrace a more pristine lifestyle. Our churches have to reach people where they are. They must deal with their cultural makeup and their socially prescribed personalities.

Television is the first of these forces to be considered. Since the thought forms of people are determined by this relatively new medium of communication, the church must learn to get people to think about the gospel in new ways that will fit these new thought forms. If people will listen only to messages that come to them through this new medium, the church has a decision to make: Is it willing to adapt its message to the configuration of a television show?

What comes across to those who receive any message is highly conditioned by the medium employed to convey that message. Television, like other communication media, is not neutral but rather distorts the *content* of the messages it transmits. Marshall McLuhan said as much when he declared, "The medium *is* the message." And so the question will have to be asked as to whether or not, when we attempt to convey scriptural things by means of television, what comes out at the other end is too distorted to be the same gospel that was delivered to us by the apostles. Perhaps the price for preaching the truth of Christ via television is that some essential dimensions of that truth get lost, simply because it is impossible for them to come across on TV.

When Malcolm Muggeridge, the English philosopher/theologian, was asked how we could use television to bring the gospel to this generation, he curtly answered, "We can't!"

Maybe Malcolm Muggeridge is right. But even if he is, that does not mean that people will not try to do it. And those who attempt to present the gospel on television *will* gather a following. Whether or not those people will be following after the biblical Jesus is something that we will have to seriously debate. Whether or not the message of the biblical Jesus must inevitably be lost via this new medium is of ultimate importance. But, regardless of what Muggeridge says, television is redefining the gospel, and we are going to have to figure out how to respond to that fact.

Second, we must pay careful attention to the ways in which our consumeristic society has created a population that seeks only self-gratification. It can be said that all human beings are self-centered as a consequence of the Adamic fall, but in every generation there have been countervailing forces that have held back the self-seeking of individuals. Religion has always been one of the primary forces.

It is a fact that the very existence of a society is dependent upon people giving up some of the things they want in order to contribute to the good of others. To that end, we have, in the past, nurtured our children to be unselfish. But in today's society, self-interest rather than self-sacrifice has been increasingly nurtured. In order to foster the kind of buying that is essential to keep our overly productive industrial economy going, individuals have been encouraged to abandon restraint and to get what is desirable for themselves, regardless of who has to suffer.

The self-indulgence of what one observer has labeled the "me generation" has changed even the religious orientation of people. As Christians, we must ask ourselves, "What kind of a gospel will attract them?" Do we yield to the marketplace and "sell" a Christianity that caters to the growing self-interest

of a commercially created culture of narcissism, or do we hold
the line and declare that only those who are willing to
sacrificially lose themselves for the sake of Christ and his
kingdom have the right to call themselves disciples?

A visit to any religious bookstore will provide ample evidence of the extent to which Christianity has capitulated to
the demands of a self-centered people. The books are, for the
most part, about how faith can serve egoistic ends. They
make Christianity into something that guarantees personal
happiness, sexual bliss, social success, and an answer to all
personal problems. The Christ who promises a cross and calls
for self-denial is hard to find in most of the best-sellers.

Should mainline churches, like the American Baptists,
face reality and redefine their message to be functionally fit
for a self-centered consumeristic society? Or should they
preach the self-surrender and sacrificial message that is so
evident in the Bible? Perhaps we have to first get people into
the church with a message that addresses their self-concerns
before we can lay on them the heavier load of what is involved
in true Christian discipleship.

Finally, we will have to ask how mainline churches should
position themselves in the midst of what James Davison
Hunter has called the "culture wars." Across America there
is a great divide between people. On the one hand, there are
those who believe that this country is experiencing an erosion
of its basic values and needs a reaffirmation of some absolute
truths that have gotten lost along the way. On the other hand,
there are those who want to liberate society so that alternative lifestyles and values they believe are fitting for a plural-
istic society can be legitimately pursued. If the mainline
churches side with the former, they will come across as trying
to force their beliefs and values on the rest of the nation. If
they take the latter position, they will seem to have embraced
a moral relativism that allows anything and everything.

What is certain is that mainline churches must decide. If
they do not, they will learn what Jean-Paul Sartre meant
when he said that not to decide is to decide. The people in

the pews are caught up in this struggle to define America; they are taking sides. And each side is vehemently crying out, "If you are not for us, you are against us." The response of the mainline churches to such a challenge will determine whether or not they have a future in the brave new world of the twenty-first century.

Chapter 4

The Television Challenge

Competing with television has been a problem for the church ever since "the tube" became part of our lives. The amount of time that we give to watching television staggers the imagination. One rather conservative estimate is that the typical American watches television five hours a day.

It is pretty obvious that having been seduced by television makes it difficult for us to give our lives to Jesus. When it comes to time, we are more committed to television than we are to service to his kingdom. Years ago, churches started dropping Sunday evening services because they were no match for Ed Sullivan, and youth leaders had a hard time getting kids away from their TV sets to attend youth fellowship meetings.

Beyond competing with TV for time, the church has to deal with the emotional commitments that people make to television. Television gets a hold on some people so that for them, the characters on television sometimes become more real and more important than their own family members.

A minister friend of mine told me a story that would have been funny had it not been so tragic. He told me about a Wednesday night prayer meeting at his church in which a woman asked for prayer for one of the characters in the soap opera she regularly watched. My friend told her, "But the people in your soap opera aren't real!"

"I know," she answered, "But the young woman I'm telling you about *is* going through a difficult time and needs our prayers."

On Super Bowl Sunday, the loss of the game by the home team can put fans into incredible fits of depression. And in homes, from the derelict dwellings of the slums of our cities to palatial mansions in wealthy suburbs, there are young mothers who pay more attention to what they see on television than what their own children are doing. There is little doubt that for too many people, television has become a preoccupation with which the church finds it difficult to compete.

Another concern about television is the values it communicates. There are those who argue that television does not so much create values as it reflects them. We've all heard the line that the media is only a mirror image of what is going on in our everyday lives. Well, I do not believe that!

Recently, the most authoritative study of sexual behavior in America gave statistical evidence that last year only 4 percent of married people committed adultery. You would never know that from television. What comes across in show after show is that everybody is doing it. When Dan Quayle attacked the Murphy Brown show because it made having a baby out of wedlock seem both commonplace and acceptable, he was greeted by a storm of scornful criticism. But Quayle was right on target, contended *The Atlantic Monthly* in a major article, and *The Atlantic Monthly* is hardly a publication noted for its conservative leanings. President Clinton, the leader of the opposition party, lent support to Quayle's opinion, saying, "I was making Quayle's speech before Quayle did."

The media doesn't reflect reality; it creates it. This is true not only about sex; it is also true about crime. The statistics show conclusively that, while there is a decline in crime in the major cities of America, you would never get this impression from talking to the American people. Most Americans, statistics to the contrary, believe that crime is on the increase and are increasingly afraid of venturing out of their homes.

Things are by no means good in America, but they are not nearly as bad as prime-time television makes them out to be.

For the church, the value orientation of television poses special problems. In the face of an overpowering media, churches find it difficult to promote the kind of sexual purity that has been traditionally preached from the pulpit. Television makes the values that prohibit premarital intercourse and demand a lifelong commitment between husbands and wives seem quaint and outdated. Modesty seems to have been totally discarded by those of us who have become used to viewing what an earlier generation would have found lewd. How do we tell young people that sexual abstinence is expected of them when they are daily bombarded by MTV videos that invite them to instant sexual gratification? How do we convince them that they should wait until marriage for sex when visual images and drumbeats constantly get their hormones flowing hot?

Less noticeable, but just as devastating to Christian values, is the affluent lifestyle that television leads its viewers to believe is their entitlement. Everyone, suggest the ads, deserves "a break today," and that break means the right to buy what the ads are selling.

Consider how the popular media are now overcoming differences that once existed between the satisfactions provided by spiritual well-being and the satisfactions that come from consumer goods. For instance, Coca-Cola (in what may have been the most famous television ad of all time) replicated the biblical imagery of the day of Pentecost. In the ad, people from various ethnic groups from around the world were assembled on a hilltop, holding hands and singing: "I want to teach the world to sing in perfect harmony." But that which creates this perfect harmony for broken humanity, overcomes the curse of Babel, unifies us, and overcomes our sense of separateness is not the Holy Spirit—it's Coca-Cola! For America, Coke has become "The Real Thing."

Think about the way the intimacy of biblical *koinonia* (fellowship) is portrayed as being created simply by buying the right kind of beer. In the now-famous ad, we are invited to be the unseen guests of some sportsmen who are having a cookout on the back porch of a rustic lodge. They have just finished a good day of fishing and are cooking some of their catch. As they pull the tops off Löwenbrau beer cans, one of them comments, "It just doesn't get any better than this." Then, as the camera pulls back to give us a good overall view of the idyllic scene, a deep baritone voice sings out, "Here's to good friends; tonight is kind of special." Through this ad, the viewers are being told that Löwenbrau beer will deliver far more than what is in the can. We are being told that the right beer can overcome the loneliness of the soul.

In our TV ads, it is as though the ecstasy of the spirit experienced by a St. Theresa or a St. Francis can be reduced to the gratification coming from a particular car, and the kind of love that Christ compared to his love for his church can be expressed by buying the right wristwatch "for that special person in your life." In all this media hype, things are sold to us on the basis that our deepest emotional and psychological needs will be met by having the right consumer goods.

In earlier times, spiritual gratification was presumed to come only via spiritual means. Thus, people could be urged to choose between the things of this world and the blessings of God. Now, that duality has been overcome. Ours is an age in which spiritual blessings are being promised to those who buy material things. The spiritual is being absorbed by the physical. The fruit of the Spirit, suggest the media, can be had without God and without spiritual disciplines. It is not simply that we are materialists who crave the goods that flood our markets, but that we are now a people who subconsciously have been made to believe that in these things we will find an end to the spiritual longings at the ground of our being.

Television certainly has had a major impact on the sexual mores and folkways of America. Messages about sexuality, often involving sado-masochism and the denigration of woman, are common fare on TV—especially on MTV. The MTV cable station brings to teenagers videos that depict orgiastic promiscuity and sexual bondage as normal modes of behavior. The impact of all of this has been overpowering and is not likely to be overcome by an occasional Sunday school lesson on a healthy and biblically prescribed sexuality. When a vice-president of MTV was asked what influence his station had on teenagers, he answered, "We don't influence teenagers—we own them."

I do not debate his contention; I only ask what it means when teenagers who are hooked on MTV say, "Jesus Christ is Lord!" Does Jesus own them or does MTV?

What is particularly depressing is the way in which television socializes preschool children. Their language, attitudes, and outlook on life are all molded primarily through television and, only to a much lesser extent, by their parents. Children have lost their imagination for play and want only to sit transfixed by the likes of Big Bird.

My son is trying to raise his children without having television as a major part of their lives, but it's hard. Their playmates and schoolmates constantly talk about what they watch on television. One day while visiting at our house, my three-year-old granddaughter piously told me, "We don't watch TV at our house because my daddy says that talking to people is more fun." Then she paused and added sadly, "But it isn't true."

What my granddaughter knew all too well is that television is easily the most entertaining thing going. Next to it, the whole world seems boring and dull. And to a generation reared on television, something has to be pretty amazing to get their attention away from the tube. The net effect on society is that nothing will be given much time or energy unless it is reduced to fun and entertainment. That goes for the news, for education, and it certainly goes for Christianity. If people are going to listen to anything, it must first be reduced to punchy and entertaining sound bites. Everything else is rejected.

Those who put on the evening news know this. Reporting

on earthquakes in Japan or hurricanes in Florida must all
be reduced to entertaining video footage with a zippy (and
probably gorgeous) newsperson providing thirty seconds of
smiling commentary. Tragedy is turned into entertainment,
and after a few short flashes of suffering, the viewer hears a
voice say, "And now this word from our sponsor."

But even the ads are not a time to turn away from the sets
to pay attention to something else. Sponsors have worked
hard to make the ads even more entertaining than the shows.
They have done their best to ensure that nobody leaves the
room to go for a sandwich or a beer.

The secret of the ads is technical changes. The best ads
throw so many images at us in such rapid succession that we
find ourselves mesmerized by what they say. A good Pepsi ad
throws out pictures of beautiful young people in a succession
of fun activities ranging from surfing and dancing to hugging
and kissing. None of the images last long enough to allow
even a trace of boredom to set in. One ad I studied put on the
TV screen sixty different images in just twenty seconds. A
Sunday morning sermon is highly unlikely to seem fast-moving by comparison.

For the most part, church leaders have gone on about their
business as though nothing has changed. Sunday morning
worship services are pretty much what they were a hundred
years ago. A glance at the average church bulletin clearly
demonstrates that what unfolds between eleven and twelve
on Sunday mornings differs very little from the usual order
of worship prescribed in a New England church at the turn
of the century. For most churches, it is as though the electronic media never happened. There is, in most churches,
such an indifference to how TV has changed the mindset of
the congregation that a social scientist would have to call it
an extreme case of a corporate denial of reality.

For those churches that have refused to face the new state
of consciousness for people socialized by television, the results have been all too obvious. The churches have experienced an erosion of attendance at Sunday morning worship

and are faced with the fact that those who do attend do so, for the most part, out of a sense of obligation. Few are those who arise on Sunday mornings to sing with the psalmist, "I was glad when they said unto me, let us go into the house of the Lord."

Perhaps church never was very exciting, but at least what happened on Sunday morning did not come across as quite so humdrum as it does nowadays. In a bygone day, stoic and prosaic worship services did not have to compete with the fast-moving excitement of television shows. The theological discourse called "the sermon" did not have to stand in contrast to the sensationalism of TV shows that use up millions of dollars to ensure that they hold people's interest.

People reared on television do not necessarily reject God or Christianity; it is just that they are lured away from them. They do not make a conscious decision to give up on the church; they simply and gradually bid it a fond farewell.

Young people are not antireligious. To the contrary, they are fascinated by the mystical side of life. When asked why they don't want to go to church, young people generally answer with one short sentence: "Church is boring!" They still like spiritual things; just note their attraction to the New Age movement. But they pay little attention to any form of religion that does not conform to the canon of entertainment prescribed by the electronic media. The fascination of the New Age movement is that it is endorsed by TV stars and thrives on music that is popularized on CDs. New Age stuff is a feeling without intellectual content. It is an instantaneous experience that requires no arduous sacrifice and demands no restraint of passion. It has perfect "functional fit," as sociologists would say, with the lifestyle of a generation that sees reality through the eyes and ears of television.

Churches that ignore all of this and go about their religious business as usual go through a gradual but very observable decline. Pulpit committees that remember "the good old days" when their churches were filled go looking for superstar preachers who will deliver spellbinding sermons that will "pack them in." These churches do not realize that they are "struggling against principalities and powers and the rulers of this age." What makes matters worse is that young preachers are usually led to believe that if they are just "good enough," they can meet such expectations. No wonder so many of them burn out and give up with a sense of having failed. Such expectations are almost always far beyond their ability to meet them.

There are others in the church who, recognizing what has happened, have assumed the attitude that "if you can't beat 'em, join 'em!" They readily acknowledge that people have changed and that the forms of religion also must change if people are going to relate to it in a positive manner. Their church, they say, has to become "user-friendly." It has to be a comfortable place for people who have grown used to a lifestyle of amusement nurtured by television. People, they claim, have a need for a church that doesn't threaten their "comfort zone," at least initially.

The very idea of having Sunday worship at 11:00 A.M. belongs to another time and another place. Eleven was a good hour when folks had to milk cows, hook up the horse and buggy, and ride for a while to the house of God. But we are not farmers anymore, and the rhythm of our lives has changed. An earlier hour for church, like 9:30, works better for both "boomers" and "busters." That way they still have most of the day left for the entertaining things that have become the focus of their lives. Some of these user-friendly churches are smart enough to plan for a six o'clock Saturday evening service. That way people can get in an hour of church and still have an evening for the movies or going out to dinner, and all day Sunday free.

I am not deploring any of this. I am simply pointing out that television has socialized us into organizing our lives around entertainment rather than work. And churches that fail to adapt to that reality don't fit into the lives of most people.

These user-friendly churches have redesigned what happens

in the Sunday (or Saturday evening) services. Instead of a traditional order of worship marked by ritualistic creeds, hymn singing, and robed choirs singing anthems, these churches offer something much more contemporary. Pipe organs are replaced by small bands including drums and guitars. Drama groups that put on short skits with a punchy message replace selections from Bach, Beethoven, and Handel. And if there is any congregational singing, it will be contemporary music with words projected on the wall instead of read from hymnbooks. The singing will be led, not by some arm-waving "beat keeper," but by a team of attractive worship leaders whom even teenagers will view as being very "hip."

Even the sermons of user-friendly churches are tailored to a TV model. The preacher, usually dressed in a sports jacket, delivers his message without notes and with no pulpit. His style resembles Jay Leno. His remarks are laced with humor and always pick up on "what's happening." The sermons are not set in the context of Scripture passages, although there are frequent Bible quotes woven into them. Instead, they are set in the context of the problems and situations of everyday life. These sermons speak, as they say, "to where people are at."

Such new churches really work. People like them and come to fill up the seats (they don't have pews!). User-friendly churches package religion in ways that appeal to those who had drifted away from church and were turned off to Christianity. The people who come are usually referred to as "seekers," and everything possible is done to make them feel relaxed. The atmosphere is a marked contrast to those old-time church services that often left folks guilt-ridden and burdened with pietistic obligations.

We should not assume that these user-friendly churches are necessarily superficial. My good friend Bill Hybels, the pastor of Willow Creek Community Church in Illinois, has modeled this new form of worship and structure. He has built around the "seeker service" an array of ministries that have discipled thousands of people into deep spirituality and social action.

At Willow Creek Community Church, where as many as twenty thousand attend their weekend services, a staff of effective ministers capably organize into Bible study groups those who are ready and willing. In these smaller, intimate gatherings, group leaders help people to spell out what most of us would consider a serious and committed Christian lifestyle. This church has been replicated across the country and even overseas, and those who imitate it often create superchurches with thousands of members. Recently, I was in Southampton, England, and found that the Willow Creek model had been replicated there with great success.

Mainline denominations seeking new ways to reach people with the gospel are taking the Willow Creek model seriously, and in many instances are using it where they start new churches. It's obvious that it would be difficult to get a long-established congregation to reject the way things have always been done on Sundays and go for this user-friendly style of church. But there are many examples where using this model in planting new churches has met with brilliant success. Usually, these new churches play down their denominational affiliations. They often use the name "Community Church" in order to have a wider appeal. Nevertheless, they hold on to their denominational affiliations, and their people participate in denominational programs. If mainline denominations are going to make a comeback, they had better take an even closer look at this model and give it wider use as they establish new churches in the many suburban communities that are springing up coast to coast.

What bothers me is that what is going on at Willow Creek Community Church is negatively criticized in some seminaries, and beginning pastors are often convinced that such forms of church life are not theologically sound but rather are sellouts to the values of the culture. I strongly disagree. I contend that such judgments are usually made on the basis of superficial observations of the seeker services. Such critics fail to consider where churches like Willow Creek Community Church take people after their initial experience.

One creative response to the need for user-friendly churches with seeker services is to have two worship services. I know of several mainline denominational churches that have added what they call a "contemporary" worship service to their Sunday schedule. Usually the nine-thirty hour is set for the user-friendly contemporary worship, followed by a traditional service at eleven. Utilizing this method, scores of churches are finding that they now have an effective means for reaching the nominally religious people who live in their neighborhoods.

The main criticism leveled at this two-service approach is that, in any given situation, we are likely to end up with two separate church bodies. The people who are part of one service become detached from those who attend the other.

This is a correct judgment. But nobody yet has explained to me why this is a bad thing. What is wrong with separate congregations, each made up of people who relate well to one another? Is this not a better option than trying to create a single worship service that creates a mishmash of what each of the groups finds desirable in worship? There are many who find traditional worship patterns a powerful and meaningful spiritual experience. Should they be asked to give up and compromise what feeds their souls for the sake of what others find relevant to their personalities? There are those who are unlikely to give the church a second look if it lacks the kind of high-energy and entertaining programs that television has socialized them to expect. Are we to ignore this reality in an effort to maintain pristine religiosity?

Those churches that have successfully initiated a second, contemporary worship service have usually eased into doing so. The most common pattern is that little by little some small study groups are established on weekday evenings. Intimacy and deep reflection in these groups build a special sense of fellowship among the members. Usually these groups call for new expressions of faith that fit with the new realities they have discovered in Christianity. It seems like a natural transition for such groups to grow into contemporary worship services. The new forms of worship seem appropriate to those whose small-group experiences have broken traditional forms.

Obviously, I am a big fan of small-group Christianity. This is because through small groups we have another creative approach for reaching those who have had their consciousness conditioned by television. This approach is marked by the sense that if you can't beat them at the game, then play a different game. Another way of putting this is to say that since we are unlikely to outdo television in our efforts to make religion entertaining, let's not try. Instead, let's try to offer something that people cannot find on TV, but which they desperately crave—*community*.

Alienation has been called a primary ailment of our times. People who live increasingly in a mass society feel cut off from intimate relationships with anyone outside their immediate families. Harvard sociologist David Riesman has called us "the lonely crowd." And the rock singer Janis Joplin sadly remarked, "I live in a world where I stand up and make love to ten thousand people—then go home and go to sleep alone."

An author once said, "How do you think you get to be a Nobel laureate? You achieve and achieve trying to get love, and then becoming a Nobel laureate is *second* prize."

Those who are into pastoral ministry often contend that it is primarily in small groups that church happens. The Holy Spirit is most likely to come, they say, when people in small groups meet in total openness to one another. They report that the awesome empowerment and excitement that happens when just a few people gather together in Christ's name seldom happens in the larger gatherings of the body of Christ (Hebrews 10:24-25).

My wife belongs to such a small group. It meets regularly and it does what church is supposed to do. That special kind of fellowship that the Bible calls *koinonia* happens there. The women in her group share their joys and frustrations at the deepest level. They learn from one another. But most important, they become persons who let Christ flow through them into one another's lives. They become mutual agents of spiritual renewal.

Such small-group experiences are an antidote to a social sickness that leaves so many of us feeling estranged and anonymous. They are biblically prescribed cures for the sense of separateness that haunts so many of us in the crowded ways of life. For those of us who are trying to figure out how to ensure the survival of the church into the twenty-first century, special attention must be given to what can be spiritually experienced in small-group encounters.

Television cannot offer the real intimacy that comes from face-to-face encounters with people who are mutually seeking God. TV tries, but fails. The producer of Madonna's videos explains that he always makes sure the camera gets close-up shots of her face so that viewers feel like she is looking right into their eyes. He says, "I want a picture that makes people think that her face is just six inches away."

But television fails. The erotic turn-ons that come from artificial intimacy cannot meet the hunger of the soul. But small-group experiences can.

I do not want to give the idea that there is anything about small-group encounters that would automatically guarantee spiritual ecstasy for the participants. Quite the opposite. Making small groups work is hard. Those who are best at it have worked at it. They have sought directions from a variety of sources. Some have studied Lyman Coleman's "Serendipity" plan of Bible study. Others have gone to seminars led by small-group expert Roberta Hestenes, the president of Eastern College. Still others have studied what Church of the Saviour in Washington, D.C., has accomplished by building its ministry around small groups.

Relational ministry, as the small-group approach is called, circumvents the effects of television by assuming that God has created us for fellowship with one another. It holds that the God whom people can encounter in intimate small-group relationships is able to break the hold television has on them, opening them to a deeper and richer life in the Spirit.

Through small groups, people come to believe that they can recover the oneness that we Baptists love to sing about on Communion Sundays:

> Blest be the tie that binds
> Our hearts in Christian love:
> The fellowship of kindred minds
> Is like to that above.
>
> Before our Father's throne
> We pour our ardent prayers;
> Our fears, our hopes, our aims are one,
> Our comforts and our cares.
>
> We share our mutual woes,
> Our mutual burdens bear,
> And often for each other flows
> The sympathizing tear.
>
> From sorrow, toil, and pain,
> And sin, we shall be free;
> And perfect love and friendship reign
> Through all eternity.[1]

Some mainline denominational pastors have made their primary ministry the development of a network of such *koinonia* groups throughout their communities. They bring these cellular units together from time to time, but it is in the small groups that they do most of their ministry.

I know of one very prominent Christian leader in New England who is considering television hookups to a network of small groups meeting in private homes scattered far and wide over the countryside. That way, solid Bible teaching could be simultaneously shared with these dispersed house churches, which then would be followed by intimate discussion and sharing within each small group of gathered people.

One thing certain is that for most people, television has made the traditional religious worship experience something that seems to belong to another era. The older generation, which came of age before television and was such a dominating influence, is dying off. And those churches that offer only the traditional forms of church inherited from the past will slowly die out. "The times, they are a-changin'!" Sociologists know that the ways in which people communicate shape the ways in which they think and the very structures of their lives. We have gone through a communication revolution. The structure of religious life that has been ours was devised for a society that was literate. That society is no more. And if mainline denominations are going to "live long and prosper," then they had better face these realities and, as Captain Kirk says,"seek out new forms of life."

But let us not leave the past completely behind. Remember that verse of Scripture in which the Lord tells us, "the kingdom of heaven is like unto a man that is an householder, which bringeth forth out of his treasure things new and old" (Matthew 13:52).

What I am trying to say was written a long time ago as part of the third verse of the old hymn *Once to Every Man and Nation*.[2]

> New occasions teach new duties,
> Time makes ancient good uncouth;
> They must upward still and onward,
> Who would keep abreast of truth.

Chapter 5

The Challenge of the Culture of Narcissism

As the church faces the challenges of the twenty-first century, it must face the fact that its message runs counter to the dominant ethos of the culture. We live in what philosopher/psychologist Christopher Lasch has called "the culture of narcissism." Contemporary Americans are self-centered in ways that defy comparison with the ways of Americans in previous generations. While egocentricity has been a problem since Eden, people used to be told that there was something wrong with it. But the "me generation," which has now taken center stage in America, has been led to believe that self-centeredness is a virtue. Such affirmations of self-centeredness come not only from the endless array of talk shows from Donahue to Oprah, but from bestselling books and pulp magazine articles. "Pop psychology" is fed to us as a daily diet wherever we turn. Whether it comes from Dr. Joyce Brothers or Dr. Ruth, we are bound to hear the message. We are told that we should look out for number one, to put our own self-actualization first, to recognize the benefits of nurturing "the art of selfishness." And always, the self-love is to come first and foremost. There is just enough truth in what we are being told to make it all sound reasonable.

The origins of this narcissistic consciousness are multiple

and complex. But near the top of the list has to be the emergence of humanistic psychology as an American pseudoreligion.

In a popular sense, humanistic psychology has become a seemingly scientific means for curing the maladies of our souls. Its simplistic remedies are more readily embraced by most of us than the biblical prescriptions that once served as answers to the problems of our lives. Of all the cures offered for the difficulties we face in everyday life, none is more common and more readily believed than the doctrine that a positive self-concept will enable us to succeed in life. No matter what the problem, we hear the same solution repeated over and over again.

If the child is not doing well in school, then all we have to do to turn that child into a brilliant student is to build up his or her self-concept.

If the teenager is to be delivered from tendencies toward delinquency, then we must make strong efforts to build up that teenager's self-esteem.

If adolescent girls are to be kept from premarital pregnancies, then we must enhance the self-concepts of those girls.

If young people are inclined towards drugs, we can enable them to escape the problems of addiction if we can just build up in them a positive self-esteem.

There is some truth to such declarations, but there is also in these statements an oversimplification. Indeed, it is healthy for young people to have positive self-concepts, but to think that nurturing a positive self-concept in them is the panacea for the deep-rooted social and psychological problems of our times is to set ourselves up for disappointment.

In order to build positive self-concepts, we have entered into an orgy of constant praise. We give out trophies for everything. We heap on rewards just for showing up. We tell kids that they are okay just as they are and that there's no need for them to exert themselves to try to prove their worth. As a matter of fact, those who do exert themselves and make great efforts to be good are looked upon as having unresolved psychological problems that make them into driven persons trying to achieve self-worth.

Recently, I heard a popular psychologist who regularly appears on TV talk shows explain that she thought that Mother Teresa was psychologically sick. She contended that Mother Teresa was suffering from a bad case of "codependency." Her analysis of this saintly woman was that she had a poor self-concept and was trying to compensate for her feelings of inadequacy by doing sacrificial service. What Mother Teresa did for others, it was argued, was an attempt to earn a sense of self-worth to compensate for her own devalued concept of selfhood. "Mother Teresa did not help the poor of Calcutta because they needed her," said this TV psychologist. "She helped them because she needed them. She needed the psychic gratification she received from serving the poor and the dying."

Such an explanation seems to me to be obscene. But beyond my own emotional reactions, such explanations are examples of the convoluted thinking that has become all too common in our narcissistic age. There is no room or justification for self-sacrifice for others in a society in which being healthy is defined as being selfish, and egocentric lifestyles are held up as the way to true happiness.

The origins of this narcissistic consciousness are multiple and complex. But at the top of the list of contributing factors has to be the emergence of humanistic psychology. The problem with all of this, in spite of whatever good it may do, is that it nurtures the culture of narcissism. It develops conceited attitudes. "There's nothing wrong with me," says our developing teenager. "I'm wonderful just the way I am."

Needless to say, the old-time religion that called young people to see themselves as sinners in need of a Savior does not play well in such a cultural milieu. A religion that is acceptable in a society imbued with this emphasis that "everybody is just wonderful the way they are" is going to have to be something other than traditional Christianity, especially in its old Calvinistic forms.

As we consider the forces that are at work creating this

culture of narcissism, we have to take special note of the part that the changing structure of the family has played in this phenomenon. With the passing of the agrarian way of life, the size of the American family began to decline dramatically. Farmers in the old days *needed* children. Children served as workhands in the everyday labors that were required to keep family farms going. They were economic assets. Every time a farmer had a child, he had somebody else to help milk the cows, plow the fields, and bring in the harvest. Given these realities, it is no surprise that the size of families was large. Lucky was the man who had a dozen children. He was on his way to getting rich.

But the role of children changed when we Americans moved off the farms and into the cities. In the modern, urban, industrial society with its laws against child labor, children are an economic liability rather than an asset. To raise a single child in the middle class, *without* paying for college, costs close to $100,000 today. We may *want* children. We may *love* children. But in economic terms, who *needs* them?

Not surprisingly, these economic realities have driven us to have smaller and smaller families. The two-child family has become the normative model.

But careful consideration has to be given to the fact that the kinds of personalities that children develop in small families are quite different from the kinds of personalities they develop in large families. In large families, the child learns to adapt to the expectations of the larger group; in a small family, the child expects the group to adapt to his or her personal expectations.

In a small family, a child leaving for school in the morning might hear Mother saying, "Darling, what time would *you* like dinner this evening?" In contrast, a child in a large family is likely to hear, "John! Dinner's at 5:30. If you're here, you'll eat." In such a system, the youngster catches on that schedules are not created to meet his or her desires, but rather that he or she had better adapt to the expectations of the larger group.

The individualized attention lavished on many children

today extends beyond the home. When the child goes off to school, the same sort of intensive focus on self is provided there. Class size has gotten smaller and smaller over the years, with the express purpose of allowing teachers to give individualized attention to each and every child.

Ours is a child-centered world. We have made a virtue out of building an exaggerated sense of self-importance in our children. Sociologists are quick to point out that ours is probably the most child-centered society in human history.

When we add up all these ingredients—a pervasive belief that our most important responsibility is to praise the growing child into success, media messages that encourage self-actualization and gratification, an economic system that requires impulse buying to survive, and small familial systems that encourage doting on children—we see the formula that is at work making ours a society of incredibly self-centered people.

What is unique to our generation is that this self-centeredness has gained theological legitimization. In other words, we are being taught that making ourselves the primary focus of our lives is what God has ordained. Whereas former generations heard thunderous admonitions from the pulpit to "forget yourself and give yourself to God and others," this generation is being led to believe that self-love is an essential prerequisite to any other kind of positive relationship.

When I was a boy in Sunday school, I learned a little chorus that reflected a value system that may be close to disappearing in our contemporary society. It went:

Jesus and Others and You,
What a wonderful way to spell joy.
Jesus and others and you
In the life of each girl and boy.
"J"is for Jesus, for he has first place.
"O" is for others we meet face-to-face.
"Y" is for you, in whatever you do,
Put yourself last and spell JOY.

Subtly and imperceptibly, we have drifted away from the attitudes expressed in that little chorus. More and more we have aggrandized the self. In contemporary religion, glorification of the self is becoming a goal, and the actualization of one's potential has been made a moral obligation.

A review of the titles of books for sale in any Christian bookstore will readily reveal that there is a growing emphasis on the self among Christian readers. The messages that call individuals to be their own best friends have moved from the secular shelves to the shelves of Christian bookstores. And should you go into a secular bookstore, you are likely to find Christian books displayed in the self-help section.

Undoubtedly, taking care of one's self *is* a Christian responsibility, but it seems that we are becoming preoccupied with it. It is easier to buy a book on how married people can have "fun dates," than it is to buy a commentary on the book of Acts. "How Firm a Foundation" is becoming better known as the title of a "Christian" aerobics program than as the title of a hymn about Jesus.

"The pursuit of happiness" is no longer just a phrase in the Declaration of Independence; it has become an American obligation. What is intriguing is the observation that we have made God into a means to achieve happiness. The achieving of personal happiness has become the purpose of life for most of us. And we have made religion into a means to gain it. For too many people, the God of love is at work in the world not so much to bring about His kingdom of justice for all, but to ensure that the individual gets all the personal happiness that he or she deserves. The churches that are "making it" are the ones that have redesigned religion to meet the spiritual hungers of an increasingly self-centered populace.

It is interesting to note the results of a recent study comparing what Japanese mothers want for their children with what American mothers want for their children. The Japanese mothers, when asked what they wanted their children to become, answered overwhelmingly, "successful." American mothers, in answer to the same question, said that they most wanted their children to be "happy." These two perspectives have very different implications. While there are no young people on earth who are more driven to succeed than the Japanese, the pressure to do well in school and to get into the premier universities is so great that those who fail often become suicidal. As I have already indicated, the American emphasis on happiness has its own negative implications.

In America, happiness for one's self is the ultimate goal, taught to us first as little children in the house. But strangely enough, that self-centered drive for happiness may be one of the primary reasons there is so much unhappiness around.

If marriages are not making us happy, we end them—in spite of the havoc divorce often wreaks in the lives of children. If we are not happy at our jobs, we quit—regardless of any commitments we have made. And if we are not happy with our churches, we simply walk away from them. For us, how happy we are determines whether or not we maintain allegiance to anything or anybody.

I grew up in an old-world Italian family. To tell the truth, I do not think my father really cared whether or not I was happy. If you had asked him, "What do you want your boy to be when he grows up?" he would have answered with one word—"good."

Is not that an almost out-of-place concept in our happiness-crazed society? To want a child to grow up "good"? It is almost an anachronism to make goodness an ultimate value for one's children.

We self-centered Americans have to be reminded that the Bible declares that it is righteousness, not happiness, that "exalteth a nation" (Proverbs 14:34). We have forgotten that truth, and we have restructured our lives so that we can justify selfishly seeking personal happiness, regardless of the consequences.

In its ugliest forms, this narcissistic emphasis expresses itself in what has been called "the prosperity theology." In a consumer-oriented economy, advertisers have convinced us that personal happiness is to be gained by buying the things they are selling. And there are those who would make God into a transcendental genie who, if we use the right words in our prayers, will supply us with the money to buy them.

A sermon entitled "God Wants You to Be Rich!" was boldly advertised on the marquee of a new superchurch. The letters of the title were two feet tall. I am fairly certain that the sermon was not about the kind of riches that we can lay up for ourselves in heaven where neither moth nor rust doth corrupt and where thieves do not break through to steal. It is as though we are saying to an America overdosed on a philosophy that the things we buy will gratify the deepest hungers of our souls: "Make Jesus your choice and you'll drive a Rolls Royce."

People have always been attracted to the pleasures of this world, and the desire to possess "things" has always been a big part of that attraction. What is unique about prosperity theology is that it legitimates this desire for things as something Christian. It is no longer a matter of choosing between seeking after spiritual riches, as the Lord urges us to do, or seeking after the riches of this world (Matthew 6:24-25). With prosperity theology, you can have both! Those who preach this version of the faith propose that becoming spiritual will make you materially wealthy. Christianity becomes the best get-rich-quick scheme that has ever come down the pike.

Ironically, there is just enough pragmatic truth in prosperity theology to make it saleable to a self-centered generation. Wealth oftentimes *is* an unintended by-product of becoming Christian. Sociologists from Max Weber to Milton Yinger have been aware of that fact. The work ethic that usually accompanies Christian discipleship is marked by honesty, good stewardship, and diligent labor. The good Christian is encouraged "to work hard in the vineyard," to render an honest day's work even when the boss isn't looking (Ephesians 6:5-6) and to wisely invest his or her earnings (Matthew 25:14-30). Such practices can often bring about economic prosperity.

Traditional Christianity does not condemn the making of wealth. Instead, it questions the accumulation of wealth and the use of it on selfish luxuries while others suffer. We are reminded of this in 1 John 3:17: "But whoso hath this world's good, and seeth his brother have need, and shutteth up his bowels of compassion from him, how dwelleth the love of God in him?"

John Wesley picks up this same theme when he tells us that a godly person "works as hard as he can; earns as much money as he can; spends as little as he can; and gives away all he can."

With prosperity theology, these calls to use whatever wealth comes your way to sacrificially alleviate the sufferings of others are ignored. Instead, the self-indulgent callously suggest that there is no point in trying to help the poor because, they point out, Jesus said "ye have the poor always with you" (Matthew 26:11). Furthermore, they argue, the poor deserve their poverty because, if they were right with God, they would not be poor. Some televangelists contend, "Prosperity is the way God rewards those who are faithful to him."

Of course the error of this kind of talk is known to anyone who has ever visited Christians in Third World countries. Those who have made such visits attest regularly to seeing people whose faith in Christ makes their own shameful by comparison, but whose economic conditions are nevertheless desperate. Godliness and prosperity do not always go together.

The frightening reality is that, in spite of biblically based arguments to the contrary, prosperity theology is being preached far and wide. And what is even more depressing is that it is gaining a wide reception. When I hear certain televangelists preach this doctrine, I say to myself, "Nobody will believe that this stuff is what the gospel is all about." But they do! Self-centered people look for a message that promises them God's help as they pursue their goals for "the good life" American style.

Prosperity theology has gained its strongest support from some variants of pentecostal Christianity. It is very attractive to America's socially disinherited. Those who have been short-changed when it comes to life's opportunities gravitate toward those churches that preach a prosperity theology.

Those who have been denied access to a materially better life or who have failed to achieve the requisites for upward mobility often seek out churches that promise socioeconomic success through spirituality.

A goodly number of superchurches have been built on the formula of prosperity theology. But it is a formula that mainline churches have, to their credit, for the most part rejected.

Many would argue that any success gained by propagating a prosperity theology is success ill-gained. It is a theology, they claim, that is diametrically opposed to all that the message of Jesus is about. They point out that while it may gain a following to declare that the blessed get rich, such a message contradicts what Jesus himself said:

> Blessed be ye poor: for yours is the kingdom of God. Blessed are ye that hunger now: for ye shall be filled. Blessed are ye that weep now: for ye shall laugh. But woe unto you that are rich! for ye have received your consolation. Woe unto you that are full! for ye shall hunger. Woe unto you that laugh now! for ye shall mourn and weep (Luke 6:20-21; 24-25).

Humanistic Psychology as Christian Theology

Middle-class people are less likely than the socially disinherited to embrace prosperity theology. They are much more likely to address their own self-centeredness with a religion that promises self-satisfaction and personal happiness through a theology that baptizes humanistic psychology.

The insights of such psychologists as Abraham Maslow, Carl Jung, and Viktor Frankl may lack empirical validation, but to the popular mind, they possess a sense of being scientific. Many social scientists, such as Paul C. Vets and Bernie Zilbergeld, have tried to make us aware that the views of these humanistic psychologists lack the character of science. While they may or may not contain some valid truths, in the end these belief systems are basically speculative philosophies. While they may parade themselves as being scientific, they really function like pseudoreligions. They promise to provide everything from love to the meaning of life. These wonderful contributions to our individualistic well-being are gained, not so much through self-sacrifice, as through the realizing of the self's potentialities. They lead us to believe that the answers to the riddles of life and the possibilities for ultimate satisfaction lie within us. Through the insights of these theories, which we are prone to think of as being scientifically grounded (after all, isn't psychology a science?), many people think they have what they need.

While pointing out that humanistic psychology is not an empirical science, I do not want to disparage what its proponents are saying to us. There is a lot of good to be derived from humanistic psychology, and what is more, many of its beliefs can easily be integrated with the Bible. That, of course, is where we find a very subtle temptation. There is a difference between what those helpful psychologists are saying and what many, myself included, believe is the message of Christ.

Those who live out the gospel often find meaning and love in life, but not always. Sometimes living out the gospel can mean suffering and rejection. While Jesus came to impart to us his joy (John 15:11), the Christian life is often marked by entering into the "fellowship of his sufferings" (Philippians 3:10). Humanistic psychology may be an array of suggestions that a self-centered people can readily employ as they try, in the words of our "pop" culture, to find themselves. But Christians are people who march to the beat of a distant drummer who calls out to us, saying: "Whosoever will save his life shall lose it; but whosoever shall lose his life for my sake and the gospel's, the same shall save it" (Mark 8:35).

Christianity has nothing against self-actualization and personal happiness; it is just that these gifts must be viewed as possible by-products of what we really should be about in our everyday lives. These blessings are not our reason to exist. They may come to those of us who faithfully commit ourselves to the ministry to which God has called us, but they are not to be the reason that motivates us into these ministries.

The theology that lies at the heart of mainline churches is a theology that defines us as a people with a fourfold calling. We are to be a *kerygmatic* people (a people who declare to a lost and dying world the Good News about the salvation Christ wrought on the cross), a *diaconic* people (a people who are committed to ministering to the needs of the hungry, the naked, the sick, and the imprisoned), a *koinoniac* people (a people who create a community that provides loving nurture to the lonely and rejected of the world), and a *prophetic people* (a people who declare the judgments of God upon all forms of evil oppression and call for the liberation of society so that it might become more like the kingdom of God).

As mainline churches consider their mission in light of the rich traditions that brought them into being, they have to decide whether or not they are willing to abandon them in order to pursue a mission that would make them more successful. They have to consider whether or not abandoning these time-honored ministries in order to render themselves more functionally fit to foster growth in membership and financial success would be worth it.

What has gotten mainline denominations into trouble over the last few decades has been their unwillingness to compromise their prophetic ministry. They stood for racial justice when such a stand was unpopular. They stood against the war in Vietnam while there was still broad popular support for pursuing that war to victory. They championed the rights of women even when patriarchal hierarchy was generally unchallenged. And as of late, they have taken bold stands against the oppression and acts of discrimination being dealt out to homosexual people.

None of these causes were initially popular, and reactions against any who embraced them were often severe and mean. While denominational leaders were voting in favor of resolutions to stand against such evils, many members of local congregations voted against them with their feet. Large numbers simply walked away from mainline churches to worship elsewhere.

There are those who would argue that mainline churches may have overdone it with their intense focus on justice issues. I have already alluded to the conclusion of many of their critics that, in their commitment to being prophetic, mainline churches have failed to fulfill their *kerygmatic* ministry and preach salvation to the lost. But when all is said and done, I am certain that history will attest to the fact that mainline churches did not play "chicken" at a crucial time in American history. They hung tough in standing up for justice. And if some say that the cost was too high, we need only ask in return, "What does it profit, if a denomination gains the whole world and loses its own soul?"

I believe that we must consider both the short-term and long-term payoffs for pursuing various missions for the church. I am convinced that the short-term effects of declaring a gospel that is a sanctified form of self-interested humanistic psychology is to gain an immediate following. Prooftexting "pop" psychology certainly has an appeal in this day and age. But I also contend that, while attractive in the "now," such a message eventually will leave people feeling frustrated and betrayed. The success that such a message can bring to the church will be short-lived when people realize that what was given was not the bread of life.

Praxis in Mission

Here I step out of my role as a journalistic sociologist and take on the role of preacher. And the message I preach is that the call of God is to sacrifice all that we are and have to the cause of God's kingdom here on earth. I believe that only those who are committed to having the Kingdom realized in history have any hope of gaining ultimate meaning for their lives and possessing the everlasting joy that has been promised by God.

Praxis is a sociological term that refers to a process wherein persons struggling to change society engage in intensive reflection. In that "reflection-in-action," they discover the truth and meaning for their lives. It is in praxis that I believe Christians are most likely to understand what their lives are meant to be and to sense the truth of God. As they work for justice for the oppressed, Christians may or may not bring about significant changes in society, but I am convinced that, in the struggles that go with this cause, they themselves will be changed.

Every summer, hundreds of college students come to work among the poor in the economically depressed communities of Philadelphia, Pennsylvania, and Camden, New Jersey. They come to serve without pay in various programs made possible by the Evangelical Association for the Promotion of Education (EAPE), the mission organization I founded in 1960. They live in crowded, uncomfortable quarters. They work day and night among some of the most disadvantaged children and teenagers on earth.

The programs of our ministry are varied. In the mornings, there are day camps for children ages six through twelve. The evenings are given over to activities for teenagers. There are sports teams, programs in the arts, tutoring programs, and a variety of cultural enrichment clubs. Through all that they do, our workers maintain a strong evangelistic witness, and during the course of the summer, many children and teenagers make decisions to become Christians. The college students who come to work with us in those programs do so with the hope of changing inner-city youngsters. But by the end of the summer, the most notable changes are in themselves.

As they work with kids, these young people are surprised by the love and joy that overtakes them. They tell me that they lie in their beds at night and reflect on the boys and girls who touched their lives during the day. As they talk with teenagers about the problems these teenagers have, our workers find themselves empathizing in ways they had never imagined possible. They gain insight into the mindset of oppressed people. They experience a consciousness raising that is more than an intellectual activity. They learn to see reality through the eyes of the poor, and in the midst of all this, they come to understand themselves as never before.

It is not a surprise to me that by the end of the summer a good number of these young collegians are radically changed. Many change their college majors and take courses of study that will prepare them for full-time Christian service vocations.

After having exhausted themselves in sacrificial service, they come to me with gratitude. In the struggles of the summer, they have come to understand the meaning of their lives and taste the joys and fulfillment that come from trying to change the world for God.

This is why mainline churches cannot and should not diminish their prophetic ministry in an attempt to become more palatable to a culture of narcissism. By involving people in the pains and sorrows that come from working for justice, endeavoring to alleviate the horrendous weight of poverty, and enduring the abuses that fall upon those who speak for people who have no voice, mainline churches will introduce their people to that which ensures spirituality. There are those who would claim that people should become spiritual *before* they act. But I believe that people become spiritual *because* they act. It is in the context of action that the kind of transforming reflection that makes us truly Christian takes place.

In Mark 10, we read the story of the rich young ruler, a young man who wanted the same rich full life that so many seek in the yogas of the New Age movement and in the directives of the experts in humanistic psychology. The young man in the story craved the quality of being that the Bible calls eternal life.

> And when he was gone forth into the way, there came one running, and kneeled to him, and asked him, Good Master, what shall I do that I may inherit eternal life? And Jesus said unto him, Why callest thou me good? there is none good but one, that is, God. Thou knowest the command-ments, Do not commit adultery, Do not kill, Do not steal, Do not bear false witness, Defraud not, Honour thy father

and mother. And he answered and said unto him, Master, all these have I observed from my youth. Then Jesus beholding him loved him, and said unto him, One thing thou lackest: go thy way, sell whatsoever thou hast, and give to the poor, and thou shalt have treasure in heaven: and come, take up the cross, and follow me. And he was sad at that saying, and went away grieved: for he had great possessions (Mark 10:17-22).

In the story, Jesus did not give him some sugarcoated words or some simplistic psychobabble. Instead, Jesus told him to *do* something. Specifically, Jesus told the rich young ruler to give away everything he had in an effort to meet the needs of the poor. Jesus explained that this was not just because the poor needed what the young man could give to them, but because the young man himself needed what would happen to him as he served the poor.

If the rich young ruler had gone through the pain and anxieties of giving up all that he treasured for the sake of needy people, he might have found what he was looking for. He might have come to grips with that which brings ecstasy to life and provides a sense of ultimate meaning in the course of the mundane.

The story ends with the rich young ruler going away sad because his great wealth had too much of a hold on him to allow him to break away and become a follower of the Lord of Lords. No course in"est," no sensitivity-training course, no self-help book, and no new theory about how to get the most out of life has the power to bestow what that young man might have gained had he gone through the process of discovery that accompanies going all the way with Jesus.

For mainline churches there might be some short-term gains in money and members that would follow restructuring the gospel message to fit the manifest requisites of people socialized into a culture of narcissism, but such a restructuring would be a denial of Christ and an invitation to a form of religiosity that would soon wear out because of its superficiality. Only those who are willing to forgo selfish ambitions and abandon the socially prescribed mania to be happy will ever discover any lasting sense of purpose in life or any sense of being grounded in the joy of living. Only a prophetic church can give people what they really need. And what they really need is not what the culture has nurtured them to want. Only a prophetic church that takes all the risks necessary to be such a church has any chance of living out the twenty-first century.

Chapter 6

The Culture Wars

James Davison Hunter argues that America is engaged in culture wars. He tells us that there are two divergent and conflicting world views operative in our society. These opposing viewpoints ask: Is ours a world governed by absolutes handed down to us from God, or do we live in a world in which an evolving humanity is given the task of ordering life according to the best insights that are available to its people? Will we live by principles laid down in the Bible, or do we try to create the principles that will guide us through our own understanding of what is best for people?

The founder of modern sociology, Auguste Comte, predicted such a conflict of world views. He taught that every society goes through stages. According to Comte, every society initially legitimates its social order theologically. By that he means that people view everything in their world as being ordained by divine powers. For those socialized into this mind-set, family life is structured according to rules laid down by God. Sexual practices are governed by revealed regulations. Even political and economic spheres are dictated by principles laid out by God from before the foundation of the world.

Eventually, contends Comte, society evolves into what he calls the positivistic stage. That is, in such an advanced society, he says, humanity recognizes that the norms that govern them are inventions of people, and that people invent those rules using logic and science.

A good illustration of the conflict between these two divergent world views can be found in the present arguments over gay and lesbian rights. On the one hand are the Bible preachers who declare loudly and clearly that gays and lesbians should be condemned for their behavior because it is pronounced as an abomination to God. Citing passages of Scripture in both the Hebrew Bible and the New Testament to support their case, they go on to say that God's laws are "from everlasting to everlasting." What was condemned in Bible times, they tell us, is just as condemned in today's world.

Over against such convictions are those who argue that the norms that guide us have to be recast in light of the times. What made sense in a bygone era may not make sense today. These so-called progressive thinkers contend that the rules about homosexuality are such a case. Modern research gives ample evidence that the homosexual orientation is not chosen. Furthermore, they argue, those who have such an orientation find little, if any, help from psychiatrists or psychotherapists. Consequently, they say, it is reasonable to assume that to construct laws that punish people for what they cannot help being and what they cannot change is cruel and unjust. A legal system that permits discrimination against gays and lesbians belongs in the same category as the legal system that once punished left-handed people because they were thought to be demon possessed. These cultural relativists declare that such a system has no place in the modern world. They are likely to say that we have evolved beyond such ignorant beliefs about homosexuality.

You do not have to go outside of Christianity to find such divergent world views. There are camps within the church that express each of the above. On the one hand, there are those who hold to a belief that with Christianity we have a progressive revelation and discovery of God's will. These brothers and sisters tell us that the Holy Spirit is constantly leading the church into beliefs and convictions that even a century ago would have been unthinkable. As examples, they point to the fact that there was a time in the not-too-distant past when slavery was viewed as reconcilable with the Bible. In our own time, they cite changing attitudes toward the role of women, especially in the life of the church, as evidence that constantly there are new discoveries of what God expects of us. God is viewed as a dynamic presence in society leading us into an increasingly liberated society wherein what was once acceptable oppression can be tolerated no more.

Those Christians who believe in this progressive revelation are led by the graduates from our more liberal theological seminaries. They are the ones who are often labeled as "modernists" and are condemned by many fundamentalists as having departed from the true faith. As you might suspect, it is the fundamentalists who hold to absolutistic beliefs and rules, which they believe remain unchanged throughout the ages. It is between these two groups that the culture wars, of which Hunter writes, are waged.

These wars have been waiting to break out for a long time. The struggles between those who believe that the Bible is a once-and-for-all revelation and those who sense a need to adapt its message to the times in which we live have been going on for decades. The conflict between these two divergent points of view became dramatically clear as far back as three decades ago when the great German-Swiss theologian, Karl Barth, went on his last speaking tour of America.

Following one of his lectures, Karl Barth permitted questions from the floor, and one of the first to stand was Carl Henry, the founder and editor of *Christianity Today*, a magazine that had become the most influential instrument for defining evangelical thinking.

As Carl Henry stood, the moderator of the meeting introduced him to Karl Barth by saying, "Dr. Barth, the questioner is Carl Henry, the editor of *Christianity Today*."

Barth answered with a quip, "Don't you mean *Christianity Yesterday?*"

To which Henry triumphantly answered, "*Yesterday—Today—*and *Forever!*"

Evangelicals tend to accuse those who reinterpret Scripture in accord with changing contexts of being cultural relativists. They say that the Word of God cannot be changed just to fit the interests of those who want to make it fit with changing mores and folkways. There is no need to *make* the Bible relevant, say the evangelicals. It *is* relevant!

There is something new, however, in what is going on between those who are engaged in such struggles. It is the shifting support toward evangelical forms of Christianity.

Whereas once the liberal thinkers who believed in the "progressive" ways of interpreting Scripture held sway over American Christianity, the power to control things has of late been taken over by the evangelical camp. During the 1950s, mainline denominations, with their somewhat liberal leaders, were the dominant forces in directing the course of American Christianity. All of that has changed during the last decade. Now evangelicals have the initiative, and there are few who would question their ability to control the contemporary religious scene. Billy Graham, not the president of the National Council of Churches, now speaks for American Protestantism. The Christian ministries that are capturing the support of the masses today, such as the Promise Keepers[1] movement for men, are evangelical to the core. Major publications such as *Time* magazine declare that this is "the decade of the evangelicals." When it comes to who is winning the culture wars within the religious community, there is no doubt that liberalism is on the defensive and that a triumphal mood persists among evangelicals.

The most dramatic takeover of a mainline denomination by evangelical forces has been the takeover of the Southern Baptist Convention. Many people would use the term "fundamentalist" when referring to the conservative faction that has come to power within the Southern Baptist Convention. I've chosen here to use the term "evangelical" because in recent years those who have formerly considered themselves fundamentalists have appropriated the term for themselves. Whether or not they have the right to do so is subject to much debate.

Many evangelicals, myself included, are upset over this development and are trying to rescue the term "evangelical" from the narrow limits it has when it is made synonymous with "fundamentalist." However, in the end, neither those of us who define "evangelical" in broader terms than the fundamentalists do, nor the fundamentalists themselves decide the meaning of the word or whom it designates. Such designation is made by the society at large. And like it or not, within the societal context of our times the word "evangelical" has come to mean "fundamentalist," with overtones that connote politically conservative views.[2]

In the Southern Baptist Convention just a decade ago, those whom the present leaders of that denomination considered liberals were in control. Evangelical leaders, such as Charles Stanley, Baily Smith, and others who pastored superchurches, were kept out of the loop of policy-making decisions. Though most of the members of local churches were evangelical in their beliefs and practices, they were being pastored by clergy who came from seminaries that were far to the left of them.

Those whom the evangelicals called "liberals" called themselves "moderates." But in a war there can be no moderates, and the evangelicals let it be known loud and clear, "If you're not with us, you're against us!"

What soon became clear is that the evangelicals were master strategists. They laid out a careful plan that required patience and diligence, and they carried out that plan in methodical fashion. Each year they made sure that they had enough votes at the annual convention of the denomination to ensure that one of their own would be elected to the presidency of the denomination. They were fully aware that the president of the denomination had the power to make crucial appointments. Specifically, the president was able to designate new members to the boards that controlled the various seminaries. The president also was in a position to appoint new members to the Sunday School Board, the

Foreign Mission Board, and the Home Mission Board.

Since these boards had only a few openings each year, it took more than a decade for the evangelicals to win sufficient control to make the changes they deemed necessary. But when they did, they wasted no time carrying out their agenda. Longtime denominational executives who were not to their liking were soon given their walking papers. Major policies that left room for "moderates" to implement their "liberal" ideas were soon changed. But the most dramatic changes were what happened to the seminaries. It took years for evangelical presidents to replace moderate board members of seminaries with evangelicals, but when the transitions were made, the results were pronounced.

One seminary after another came under the scrutiny of the evangelical boards. New presidents were appointed to govern these schools, and each had a mandate to weed out liberalism. The doctrine of the inerrancy of Scripture had to be upheld, and any who could not comply with it would have to leave the faculty. In seminary after seminary, professors who had served long and faithfully were forced to leave because their views did not match evangelical requisites.

In the case of Southwestern Theological Seminary in Fort Worth, Texas, the president, Russell Dilday, was dismissed in an autocratic manner that many contended violated the due process for such a move. Consequently, the national accrediting body for seminaries, the Association of Theological Schools of the United States and Canada, is considering taking accreditation away from the school.

In the case of Southwestern Theological Seminary, the decision to oust the president was not even because of his views. Actually, Dr. Dilday was sufficiently evangelical in his theology to pass any orthodoxy test that the new board members could throw at him. He had to go, so far as they were concerned, because he was a man who had a conciliatory attitude towards the moderates in the convention. Dr. Dilday, though an evangelical himself, wanted there to be room in the denomination for those who held more liberal views. In a war there is no place for the slightest sympathy for the enemy, and the evangelicals definitely had declared war on the opposition.

Along with leadership changes, there were also significant changes in the official positions of the denomination on a variety of beliefs and practices. Whereas the denomination once allowed for those with pro-choice beliefs about abortion to be welcomed and affirmed within it, the new regime demanded a commitment to a pro-life position. This was especially evident in the attitudes of its leaders towards both former President Jimmy Carter and President Bill Clinton.

Both of these presidents (who hold membership in Southern Baptist churches) believe that abortion should not be declared illegal. In taking such a stance, they were very much within what was permissible according to a change in the bylaws passed by the Southern Baptist Convention in 1982. But that resolution was passed before the evangelicals took over, and the new leaders strongly endorsed the pro-life position held by most members in Southern Baptist churches. When leaders of the Southern Baptist Convention went to the White House, they exercised what they believed was their prophetic obligation and called upon President Clinton to repent of his pro-choice policies.

Certainly, negative attitudes towards gay and lesbian rights became pronounced under the new leadership. Binkley Memorial Baptist Church in Chapel Hill, North Carolina, and Pullen Memorial Baptist Church in Raleigh, North Carolina, became ostracized from the Southern Baptist Convention because they admitted practicing, monogamous, homosexual couples into membership. Resolutions on both the national and state levels addressed the homosexual issue. While these resolutions did not condemn those who had a homosexual orientation, they were clear and strong in their condemnation of any behavior that included genital contact between homosexual partners. There is little doubt that any forms of physical affection between gays or between lesbians would be taboo for those who wanted to maintain good standing within Southern Baptist circles.

But the culture wars went beyond the debates on abortion and homosexuality. They also included attitudes toward women. Although the ordination of women was well on its way to becoming a *fait accompli* within the SBC, the new leadership suddenly began to question the practice. They said that it was not as if there was no place for women in ministry within the SBC, but it was just that they were calling for adherence to the teachings of the apostle Paul who said: "Let the woman learn in silence with all subjection. But I suffer not a woman to teach, nor to usurp authority over the man, but to be in silence" (1 Timothy 2:11-12).

There is no question but that over the years women have served as preachers and missionaries for Baptists. But the new leaders of the SBC contend that unfaithfulness to the teachings of Scripture in days gone by is no excuse for continuing the practice. The Bible is not to be reinterpreted, they would argue, to fit a social context highly influenced by feminist politics and thinking.

What has happened within the Southern Baptist Convention has given encouragement to evangelicals in other denominations. The Good News movement is trying to bring about similar changes within the United Methodist Church. The Presbyterian Lay Committee is at work towards the same ends within the Presbyterian Church (USA). A similar organization within the Episcopal church, Episcopalians United, is committed to the same goals. Evangelicals are on a roll, not only within the Southern Baptist Convention but in every denomination, and there seems to be no stopping them. Sociologists always knew that beneath the liberal pronouncements that gave a face to mainline Protestantism lay a reservoir of evangelical Christians committed to the fundamentals of the Christian faith. What has surprised most observers is their capacity to organize and to begin taking over decision making in mainline denominations. If we are to understand what is going on in Protestant Christianity, it is important that we know more about evangelicalism—

where it came from, how it differs from old-time fundamentalism, where it is headed and what dangers it faces. It is to such questions that we must now turn our attention.

The Time of Evangelicalism in America

Since approximately 1965, evangelicalism has demonstrated a dramatic rise. For more than a quarter of a century, this movement within Christianity has shown a vitality and growth pattern that has moved it from the periphery of American Christianity to center stage. However, in the process of going through this passage from marginality to becoming the dominant force in contemporary Protestant religion, evangelicalism has itself undergone significant changes.

Originally, evangelicals defined themselves in relationship to fundamentalists. They claimed to hold the same theological stance as fundamentalists, but they rejected the sectarianism and subcultural practices of their fundamentalist brothers and sisters. The following excerpts from the doctrinal statement of Eastern College, where I teach, reflect the conservative theology of evangelicals as well as any summary of their beliefs that I might offer.

> We believe in the unity of God's truth, whether supernaturally revealed or humanly discovered, and we value the search for knowledge and understanding in all areas of life. We are guided by our faith in Jesus Christ who is "The way, the truth and the life."
>
> We recognize the Bible, composed of the Old and New Testaments, as inspired of God and as the supreme and final authority in faith and life. We submit ourselves to carrying out our mission under its authority and seek to apply biblical principles to all facets of human aspiration and action.
>
> We affirm the importance of calling all persons in this country and around the world to personal faith and faithful discipleship in following Jesus Christ as Savior and Lord. We intend for every student to have a meaningful and appropriate opportunity to hear and respond to the call for repentance, faith and obedience to Jesus Christ.

Fundamentalism arose in America during the first half of the twentieth century as a reaction to the modernist thought that was coming out of Europe, and especially Germany. At that time, higher and lower biblical criticism, as expressed in Graf-Wellhausen's theory of Scripture, seemed to be undercutting the authority of Scripture.

By the 1950s there were those who viewed the Scriptures as mythological embodiments of truth without much, if any, historical grounding. During this period neo-Hegelian theologies replaced the belief in a transcendent God with doctrines that made God an immanent and impersonal force that was driving both history and humanity to higher levels of development.

The doctrine of evolution challenged the long-held belief that God had created the *cosmos* and humanity in six 24-hour days. Social Darwinism gave the impression that human society was caught up in a developmental process that would produce a kingdom without sin through a savior without a cross. The new humanity and the kingdom of God were defined by the modernists as the inevitable consequences of dynamic forces that were already at work within human history.

In opposition to this overly optimistic view of history that heralded a new era of perfectibility, fundamentalists declared an alternative theology. To them, the old-time doctrine of original sin was still a binding truth. Contrary to the modernists, the fundamentalists believed that sin had had a cumulative effect since Adam and Eve and that humanity was getting more and more evil. Fundamentalists did not believe that perfectibility for humanity and society was just around the corner. The hope for the world, they argued, was nothing less than the premillennial return of Christ. In their eyes, the world was getting worse and worse every day and only the Lord's return could halt this inevitable spiritual and moral disintegration of humanity.

Salvation, for the fundamentalists, was not the result of some divine presence driving the historical process to higher and higher levels of perfectibility. Instead, it was an act of a transcendental God who, through His Son's death on a cross, provided deliverance for the elect. Most of humanity, the fundamentalists believed, was doomed to eternal damnation. But the few who trusted in Jesus as personal Savior would be saved and caught up to heaven to be with God the Father. As for this terrestrial world, it would be consumed by the fire of God's judgment.

The Bible, according to the fundamentalists, was literally true, word for word. They affirmed many doctrines that modernists had tossed aside in cavalier fashion. Doctrines such as the virgin birth, the deity of Jesus, and belief in the miracles and the bodily resurrection of Jesus were the core of their theology.

Against the onslaught of scholarship coming from the modernist camp, fundamentalists kept the faith. They believed that the old-time religion that had been good enough for their fathers and mothers was good enough for them. Today, they might be ridiculed by some as being anti-intellectuals, but they did hold the fort for orthodoxy until intellectual reinforcements could come to the rescue. They kept the modernists from sweeping away completely the beliefs of traditional Christianity.

Under the blistering attacks coming from modernists, the fundamentalists eventually made separation and escape a primary strategy. Over and over they would recite to their people the Pauline scriptural passage: "Wherefore come out from among them, and be ye separate, saith the Lord, and touch not the unclean thing; and I will receive you, And will be a Father unto you, and ye shall be my sons and daughters, saith the Lord Almighty" (2 Corinthians 6:17-18).

And separate they did!

They pulled their young people out of secular colleges and universities, fearing that their youth would be swayed away from Christ by the impressive sophistication of worldly professors. They set up colleges of their own so that their young people could get an education in the context of a learning

community that respected "The Word of God." Fundamentalists set up their own seminaries to insure that there would
be a clergy devoid of what they believed to be the heresies of
modernism. And as mainline denominations became perme-
ated with leaders whom they considered to be in the modernist
mold, fundamentalists even pulled their churches out of the
membership of mainline denominations.

In the case of the American Baptist Convention, some of
these separated churches joined groups like the General
Assembly of Regular Baptists. Some formed a new denomination named the Conservative Baptist Association. Other
mainline denominations had similar split-offs of groups of
churches that formed separate denominations committed to
historical orthodoxy. Many congregations simply established
themselves as independent fundamentalist churches and
proudly declared that they had no allegiance to any authority
beyond their local congregations and the Bible.

Fundamentalism, with its separatist orientation, eventually
became more than just a countervailing theological movement
against modernism. Over the years it became a subculture.
Like other subcultures, it developed a set of beliefs, values,
and practices that seemed, to those who were not a part of it,
strange and out of step with the modern world. Behavioral
expectations that included taboos on smoking and alcoholic
beverages became part of the fundamentalist value system.
Dancing was included on the list of prohibitions, as were
movies, except in their most wholesome expression. At times,
fundamentalism seemed to be more defined by its rules and
regulations than by anything else. But regardless of their
legalistic tendencies, the fundamentalists must be credited
with not letting American Christians forget that bringing
people into a "born again" experience is central to the mission
of the church.

There could be little doubt that, in their enthusiasm for
bringing in the Kingdom, the modernists considered the task
of converting people an outdated emphasis for the church. In
reality, they had strong doubts that radical personal conversion

was even necessary. Caught up in the optimism that pervaded the American mind in the first part of the century, they tended to believe in the innate goodness of humanity. Sin, they contended, was the consequence of people having to live in unjust and oppressive social arrangements. Poverty, racial prejudice, imperialism, class conflicts, and ignorance, they declared, set people up to behave in destructive ways. The modernists believed that by changing the institutional structures of society and by eliminating the social conditions that generate sin, they would eliminate the causes of sin and produce an essentially good human race. The call of God, for them, was to participate in God's efforts to restructure society so that the positive potentialities of people would emerge and dominate behavior.

This approach to salvation came to be known as the Social Gospel, and the fundamentalists reacted against it with vehemence. They would have absolutely nothing to do with making social action any part of what they believed Christianity to be all about.

Looking back on those times gives us a sense that modernism was extremely naive about the human condition. But it must be remembered that modernist theology was a reflection of an era in which Americans went off to war in Europe believing that they were going to fight the war that would end all wars. They believed they could build unsinkable ships and that progress was the inevitable consequence of science.

The voices of such theologians as Karl Barth in Germany and Reinhold Niebuhr in the United States were yet to have their impact on mainline church thinking. Talk of the radical nature of our personal sinfulness and the belief that the pervasiveness of evil in our lives made human efforts to achieve social perfectibility a pipe dream were not yet part of sophisticated conversation. The religious intelligentsia prior to World War II tended to believe that every day in every way we were getting better and better and better.

If modernism was plagued with a naive optimism concerning human nature, fundamentalism was afflicted with a

pessimistic understanding of society and had little hope for
any good ever being accomplished in this world. Whereas
modernists saw everything coming up roses, fundamentalists saw nothing but the growing perversity in society. Fundamentalists looked around and saw humanity in decline.
They saw a working out of an inevitable disintegration of
anything good within the human race. Evil, they believed,
was becoming dominant in what they called the "last days"
and nothing could stop it.

Social action programs, as far as the fundamentalists were
concerned, were nothing more than the rearranging of the
deck chairs on the *Titanic*. In their opinion, society was going
down the tubes, and the only reasonable thing for the church
to do was to rescue as many people as possible from the fate
of eternal damnation before this world came to an end. The
future, they believed, was hopeless as far as positive social
change was concerned. This world was passing away, and in
the face of impending doom, fundamentalists believed that
the church should concentrate its efforts upon getting people
ready for the next world, rather than trying to fix up this one.

It is easy to figure out how such a reaction against the
social agenda of the modernists led fundamentalists to disengage from anything that looked like an attempt to reform
social structures or ameliorate the progress of humanity. But
in their overreaction against modernism, fundamentalists
turned their backs on the justice issues that are an integral
part of the Bible they love so much. They did not pay attention to the call of the prophets to stand up for the poor and
the oppressed. They failed to see the implications for racism
and sexism in such Pauline passages as Galatians 3:28:
"There is neither Jew nor Greek, there is neither bond nor
free, there is neither male nor female: for ye are all one in
Christ Jesus." And they seemed almost to ignore the dictates
of the Sermon on the Mount (Matthew 5-7).

Some fundamentalists, especially those who made the
footnotes of the Scofield Reference Bible the basis of their
theology, assigned the ethical requisites of the Sermon on the

Mount to an age that would come with Christ's return. The ethical principles laid down in Matthew 5-7 were far too radical to be applied to our present society, as far as they were concerned. Only in the world to come, wherein those who were perfected in Christ would live, could the utopian society that Jesus preached be implemented. These fundamentalists contended that any effort to improve society based on these principles prior to his return would be doomed to failure. Almost all fundamentalists held in common the belief that social concerns were not to take up the time and energy of the church. Saving lost souls was what we were to be about.

As the decade of the sixties broke upon America, fundamentalism seemed more than a little detached from what was going on in the world. It was the era of the civil rights movement. The war in Vietnam had generated a massive antiwar movement. Lyndon B. Johnson had raised the hopes of the underclass of the nation with his promises of the Great Society. The Peace Corps was generating visions of social idealism among a generation of young people who were awakening from the lethargy of the fifties and looking for ways to do good in the world.

Little of this seemed relevant to what the church should be about, as far as most fundamentalists were concerned. But there were those among them who felt somewhat uneasy with this detachment from the challenges presented by the social movements of the times. There were some fundamentalists who believed that the Bible provided imperatives for engaging in what was happening in society, and contended that commitment to social justice was required as part of Christian discipleship.

It was Carl Henry, a prominent American Baptist scholar, who gave a voice to this increasingly socially conscious group of onetime fundamentalists who eventually came to be known as evangelicals. Henry was into traditional theological orthodoxy, but he was also conscious of the shortcomings of fundamentalism. He was especially disturbed that, in their overreaction to the theology and agenda for the church outlined by

modernists, fundamentalists had turned their backs on social concerns.

Evangelicals became convinced that when it came to the
evils of this world, fundamentalism was majoring in minors
with its legalisms and had overlooked some weightier concerns such as racism and poverty. These dissidents also
deplored the anti-intellectual attitudes of fundamentalism
and believed that the time had come to engage the secular
academics in serious debates.

There were many ways in which evangelicals differenti-
ated themselves from fundamentalists, but none was more
important than their attitude toward Christian social action.
Whereas fundamentalists tended to write off this world and
reject invitations to work for social change, evangelicals
found in Scripture a call to transform society. They did not
buy into the naiveté of the modernists who believed that the
kingdom of God was realizable through human enterprise and
effort. They recognized that evil would not be eradicated from
society without divine intervention at the Second Coming of
Christ. But between now and the Second Coming, they believed that they could win battles for causes of social justice.
They believed that God, through the church, was initiating
a transformation of the world. The church would not complete that transformation, but at the Second Coming, Christ
would come and make our feeble efforts a part of his triumph
in history—"Being confident of this very thing, that he which
hath begun a good work in you will perform it until the day
of Jesus Christ" (Philippians 1:6).

To best understand the evangelicals' view of what was
going on in the world, we can look to how they interpreted
one of Christ's most prominent parables, found in Matthew
13:24-30.

> . . . The kingdom of heaven is likened unto a man which
> sowed good seed in his field: But while men slept, his
> enemy came and sowed tares among the wheat, and went
> his way. But when the blade was sprung up, and brought
> forth fruit, then appeared the tares also. So the servants

of the householder came and said unto him, Sir, didst not thou sow good seed in thy field? from whence then hath it tares? He said unto them, An enemy hath done this. The servants said unto him, Wilt thou then that we go and gather them up? But he said, Nay; lest while ye gather up the tares, ye root up also the wheat with them. Let both grow together until the harvest: and in the time of harvest I will say to the reapers, Gather ye together first the tares, and bind them in bundles to burn them: but gather the wheat into my barn.

For evangelicals, the wheat symbolized the kingdom of God. The good that God is accomplishing by building just institutions and creating a people obedient to God's will is demonstrated as the wheat grows and develops right up to the final day of judgment.

But this optimistic view of the kingdom of God growing towards fruition is counterbalanced in the parable by the reminder that the Evil One is also at work in the world. The growth of the tares symbolized, for evangelicals, that Satan is creating his own evil enterprise.

Evangelicals believed that the two kingdoms have grown up side by side throughout history. Those who were overly optimistic about the triumph of the kingdom of God, as the modernists tended to be, were warned through the parable that there is a demonic kingdom that would grow and assert itself until that final day when Christ returns. On the other hand, those who tended toward an overly pessimistic view of what could be achieved in human history, as was the case with fundamentalists, were reminded that God's kingdom was alive and well and growing.

It is this balance that evangelicals made central to their understanding of history. And it was this view of what was possible and expected between now and the Day of the Lord that enabled them to enter into efforts to change the world without unrealistic hype.

Evangelicals would not be sucked into believing that Utopia was a possibility through human achievement. Nor would they be deluded into thinking that there was no possibility for progress towards justice. Knowing their limitations, they could participate in efforts to change the world because, while they knew they could not complete the task of Kingdom building, they also knew that they could not be defeated. The church, they believed, would not limp out of history a battered, beaten, ragtag army. Instead, it would be joined by its Lord, who would lead them to a climatic triumph over evil. They preached that the good work that God had initiated in their own feeble efforts to create a society marked by justice and love would be brought to completion when the trumpet of the Lord was sounded to end this present age.

It was this balance of evangelicalism that attracted so many people into the movement. Evangelicals were a people who, while committed to bringing others into a conversion experience with Christ, still recognized the biblical call to social justice. They held to biblical absolutism as opposed to any semblance of "situational ethics." But they did so without getting into the oppressive legalism that had haunted so many of those who were into rigid fundamentalism.

As evangelicalism grew, it developed programs that became some of the most brilliant organizational and promotional instruments imaginable. Specialized organizations such as Young Life and Youth for Christ reached into high schools and touched the lives of teenagers in ways that those in charge of denominational youth programs had never dreamed of implementing. Prison Fellowship, founded by Chuck Colson, developed into a ministry that reached into almost every prison in America. New organizations such as World Vision and Compassion International found ways of meeting the needs of people in Third World countries with an effectiveness that those who headed up world relief in traditional denominations found amazing.

When it came to promoting their cause, evangelicals proved to be communication geniuses. They created Christian radio stations by the hundreds and even founded television networks of their own. Evangelical presses such as Word, Zondervan, and Nelson soon edged books published by mainline denominations off the shelves of the bookstores. Evangelicalism was on a roll, and its rhetoric about transforming America for Christ began to sound a triumphal note, as evangelical concerns were beginning to be expressed in programs and actions.

By the early 1970s, there was evidence that evangelicals were about to make the bold move of directly confronting the American political system in order to bring it into accountability with their own biblical convictions. Two things got them started. First was the *Roe* v. *Wade* decision of the Supreme Court to make abortion legal. Second was the election of Jimmy Carter as president of the United States.

The legalizing of abortion was, to most evangelicals, the legalizing of the murder of innocent infants. It was a concern too great to be ignored. Politics might once have been something that concerned only those liberal Christians who were into the social gospel, but with *Roe* v. *Wade*, evangelicals woke up to the realization that they themselves had to get politically involved. They believed that if they were going to save America from an evil they equated with the Holocaust, they would have to organize themselves as a political action group. This thinking gave birth to Jerry Falwell's Moral Majority movement.

Jimmy Carter added fuel to the fire that was being kindled across America when he called the White House Conference on the Family. While running for president, he had pointed out the need for this country to strengthen and even rebuild the disintegrating families of the nation. He believed that the family was the basic institution of society, and that our failing family system would sooner or later spell disaster for America's hopes for a better future.

When the conference was called, things happened that no one had expected. Everybody from radical feminists to civil rights advocates had been invited, and the heated discussions that ensued produced nothing except the realization that the traditional family system so revered in American folklore was under attack. There seemed to be no way to come to a consensus on anything, not even a definition of what constitutes a family. Did people cohabitating without being legally married constitute a family? Were teenage mothers and their children born out of wedlock considered to be families? And finally, were gay and lesbian couples to be considered married and entitled to raise children as families?

It was the issue of homosexual marriages and the designating of them as legal families that set off intensive reactions across America. And it was the evangelicals who took up the cause of challenging what was coming out of the White House conference.

Mainline denominations, with their somewhat liberal leaders, were not particularly upset by all of this. The fact that they were not upset, upset the people in the pews and got them wondering if their denominational churches were really where they ought to be. The nondenominational evangelical churches eagerly welcomed those who were disaffected with mainline denominations. It was these same churches that were destined to be part of a growing political movement that has become larger and more influential than Jerry Falwell's Moral Majority. Today these churches are, for the most part, included under the label of the Religious Right.

It has been said by a great philosopher of history, that whom the gods destroy they first make drunk with power. It may be that the immense power gained by the Religious Right will prove to be its undoing. As the Religious Right flexes its great political muscles, it frightens many people. What once was regarded as a positive Christian voice on the American scene is increasingly viewed by many as a threat to what makes our democracy work. There is a growing concern that the Religious Right is becoming a movement that uses political power to impose on the rest of society its particular vision of what America should be.

With the election of Bill Clinton, the Religious Right has skyrocketed to prominence. The November 1994 elections clearly demonstrated that this group has the power to shape the future of our country. Concerns about its conservative political agenda, which some consider to be extremist, have led many of those who had left mainline denominations for evangelical churches to begin to consider what they have gotten themselves into.

What makes matters worse in the minds of many are the relentless attacks of some of the leaders in the evangelical community on President Clinton. Instead of dealing with the issues that concern evangelicals, such as abortion, the rights of gays and lesbians, and the role of religion in the public sector, some leaders have resorted to denigrating the president's character. In their attack, they have not been above spreading rumors, telling lies, and engaging in slander.

Perhaps the most notable example of this negative campaigning has been the selling of *The Clinton Chronicles*. This is a set of videotapes that allege that the president has been involved in murdering his political opponents, running a drug ring out of Little Rock, Arkansas, and being a cocaine addict himself. At the time of this writing, more than 100,000 copies of these videos have been sold at forty dollars apiece. Undoubtedly, an even greater number will be sold as the 1996 campaign for the White House gets under way.

A reaction is beginning to set in. To many, the outrageous accusations on these tapes have the marks of an out-of-control political movement. Others sense that some of the tactics employed by extremists could lead to an oppressive government in the future.

All of this is having its effect upon the Christian community. It may be that those who were once all too ready to leave their mainline churches because they felt themselves being dragged into radical politics when they really wanted the church to minister to their spiritual needs may be equally uneasy in their new religious home. These people may be looking for an alternative to their evangelical churches now that these churches are becoming increasingly politicized with extreme and radical rhetoric. Mainline denominational churches may be looking a lot better to a large number of people these days.

Chapter 7

The Beginning of the Counterattack

The November 1994 election was a wake-up call. The Republicans swept into control of both the House and the Senate, and their victory was also a major triumph for the Religious Right. To a great extent the Republicans owed this incredible victory to them.

Talk shows on religious radio stations, largely reflecting the values of the Religious Right, have been acknowledged by many analysts to have been a major factor in determining the outcome of that election. *USA Today* reported that for 38 percent of the voters, religious concerns (largely generated by the Religious Right) had strongly influenced the way in which people cast their ballots. It was generally conceded that the Religious Right, primarily led by the Christian Coalition, had seized control of eighteen of the Republican state party organizations, and that there was ample evidence that these same forces had become a powerful presence in most of the others. Consequently, the victory of the Republicans in the November 1994 election was broadly admitted to be a victory for the convictions of the Religious Right. On the state level, the party platforms of the Republicans reflected these values, beliefs, and concerns.

The Wednesday morning after that election, the sun shone

brightly on the fortunes of the Religious Right, and to many this was a sign that they were winning the culture wars. Those Christians who espoused more moderate political policies and who were concerned that reactionary religiosity was becoming more and more evident throughout American Christianity realized that the Religious Right was not a bad dream that would pass away or a fad that could be ridiculed into obscurity. Something had to be done—and fast. The troops to oppose this growing army of what the moderates believed were sanctified right-wingers had to be recruited. Somebody had to do something to unify the dissenting voices that remained and mold them into a dynamic countervailing force.

Already some of the leaders of the National Council of Churches had formed an organization to oppose the growing power of the Religious Right. But to many in the mainstream of American Christendom, the NCC had the reputation of being so radically liberal that it was considered to be little more than a voice crying in the wilderness. These mainstream Christians viewed traditional liberalism, both in its theological and political forms, as being bankrupt of answers for the problems of their times. Any organization put together by the National Council of Churches would be viewed as more of the same.

There was a need for the broad-based community of basically orthodox Christians that could be found both in mainline denominations and in the progressive wing of evangelicalism to establish a common cause. Mainstream Christians needed to come together and lay out a plan, not only to stand up to the encroaching power of the Religious Right, but to save the church from being labeled as a reactionary institution for years to come. It was absolutely necessary that whatever action this group took be clearly distinguished from the liberal Christianity of past decades. It had to be proactive, not simply reactive. It had to herald a positive alternative to the two sides that stood opposed in the culture wars. It had to offer a balanced alternative to those who could identify neither with the liberalism often found in the extremes of mainline denominationalism and the left wing of the Democratic party, nor with the politics and theological triumphalism of the Religious Right.

Jim Wallis, the editor of *Sojourners*, was the one who called the meeting. Some of us had waited for an individual who was more "politically correct" to step forward and sound the call to stand up to the Religious Right. Jim Wallis and his magazine had the reputation of being theologically evangelical, but his somewhat left-of-center political views were often seen as being outside the mainstream of the evangelical community. However, the more moderate leaders in the evangelical ranks who might have been more "politically correct" seemed reluctant to take on the responsibility.

The stakes were high. The Religious Right had gained the power to break the careers of anyone who crossed them. They were a dominating presence within the National Religious Broadcasters. Through the thousands of Christian radio stations and the Christian television networks that were members of the NRB, they could "puff" would-be leaders into national prominence or, just as easily, destroy their credibility.

The Religious Right also had control of countless Christian newspapers, magazines, and periodicals that, for better or worse, were opinion-formers for church people across the nation. Consequently, evangelical leaders who did not buy into the agenda of the Religious Right were reluctant to do anything that would make them look like voices of dissent. Fear was a reality for many.

Jim Wallis had no need to work overtime trying to keep in the good graces of right-wing televangelists and the leaders of the Christian Coalition. He had no organizational religious empire to preserve. He didn't have to play it safe with would-be contributors. Wallis's Sojourner Community in Washington, D.C., didn't depend on mail-in contributions from people that he dare not offend. Perhaps it would have been better if some less controversial evangelical leader had sounded this clarion call. But the fact was that, whether for fearful caution or some other reason, none of those leaders did. And so it was the maverick Jim Wallis who stepped up and said, "Let's get together and get organized."

The original meeting called to organize this "movement of the center" was modest by any standard. Joe Hacala came as a very unofficial representative of the Roman Catholic Bishops' council. He was worried about the growing influence of the Religious Right within Roman Catholicism. He was concerned about how the social platform and the community development work he was into might be affected by the changing political climate that was sweeping the nation.

Marian Wright Edelman of the Children's Defense Fund was at the meeting. She was concerned about what the political agenda of the Religious Right would mean to the struggling mothers and children who were the focus of her ministry. Changing attitudes toward welfare, specifically toward government programs for dependent children, troubled her. She felt that the close alliance between the Religious Right and those Republicans who were advocating the "Contract With America" did not bode well for those children who had been victimized by birth. As Newt Gingrich called for a rebirth of orphanages, she wondered what the future held in store for such children.

Eugene Rivers, a minister from Boston who attended that first meeting, expressed the concerns of many African American Christians. He had grown up in the ghetto and had struggled long and hard to stand up to the racism that had psychologically and socially crippled so many African American young people. As the Christian Coalition had become overtly allied with the conservative Republican agenda, he had worried about what would happen to his people. With the Christian Coalition contributing a million dollars to Newt Gingrich, specifically to promote the "Contract With America," Rivers believed that there was a new force to be reckoned with in his struggle. He wondered whether the advances made for African Americans with a Democratic Congress were going to be lost.

Eugene Rivers talked about how the Religious Right was cleverly moving to seduce the black bourgeoisie into its movement. He was concerned that eventually the movement would co-opt the black middle class, turning them against the urban underclass African Americans who had been shut out of the American Dream.

And there was Tony Campolo. I had a vested interest because I had already taken a lot of "hits" from the Religious Right for my nonconformity on a variety of social issues. I was part of the progressive wing of the evangelical community and, as society at large seemed to identify us with the Religious Right, I wanted to make sure that evangelicalism was delivered from this marriage. Jesus is neither a Democrat nor a Republican. I wanted to make sure that the world at large saw the Christ of evangelicalism as being above either of these parties, judging both the Democratic Party and the Republican Party according to principles of justice laid out in God's Word.

That first meeting, held in Washington, D.C., did not accomplish much, but it did allow the five of us to voice a common agreement that the time had come to act. Jim had just finished a speaking tour his publisher had arranged to promote his new book, *The Soul of Politics*. Everywhere he had gone, he had encountered large numbers of people who were ready to "move" and be a part of a new religious movement in America. Over and over again he had been asked whether evangelicals had any organizational alternative to the Religious Right. People complained that nobody was calling for the creation of a movement that would work out evangelical convictions in a way that would transcend the polarities of the old political left of liberal Christianity and the new Religious Right, which seemed to be swallowing up evangelical Christianity. I added a note of encouragement to the meeting because in my travels I had been hearing the same things Jim reported hearing.

A couple of hours went by as we described for each other what we had observed and learned about the strategy of the

Religious Right. We talked about how its key leaders had come together at a round-table meeting and established a program that would enable them to carry their program to the American people and change the American religious and political landscape. We reflected on how those who were at that meeting had established a division of labor, giving to each member specific assignments that would blend together into an overall scheme for success. The brilliance, thoroughness, and effectiveness of the program of the Religious Right forced us to give them grudging admiration.

Jim suggested that if we were going to make a legitimate attempt to give the Religious Right a run for their money, we needed not only to imitate their methods, but to beat them at their own game. We had to figure out ways to organize on the grass-roots level that would mobilize opinion in favor of new forms of progressive Christianity.

Unlike the Religious Right, we had no desire for our group to be an official player in American politics. We only wanted to exercise a presence in the church. Our concern was to keep evangelical Christianity from being co-opted by movements like the Christian Coalition. We had a commitment to become what we considered to be a progressive voice, not only in organizations like the National Association of Evangelicals (NAE), but in each and every denomination in America. We had no desire to become to the Democratic Party what the Religious Right had become to the Republican Party. What concerned us was that there be an evangelical movement that would stand above these cleavages and call for both parties to build on the gains that had been made by progressive Christians in their struggle to maintain a primary emphasis on evangelicalism while strongly advocating the rights of women, the dignity of homosexuals, the demilitarization of the world, an end of racism, and a war on poverty.

Jim argued that we had to find ways to make the kind of Christian value system we were advocating something that people would talk about when they took coffee breaks, assembled at water coolers, met for dinner, and had discussions in their Sunday school classes.

But before any of that could happen, something else had to take place. We had to bring together fellow believers from across America in order to discuss and answer the question, What is it that we have in common? We were Catholics and Protestants. We were from long-established denominations as well as from the new progressive wing of evangelicalism. We were of different races, genders, and economic classes. Yet, in spite of our diversity, we sensed a certain oneness of spirit. We had to figure out how to articulate to a waiting evangelical community what it was that created that sense of unity.

As you can imagine, such a meeting was an opportunity for us to give vent to the frustrations each of us was feeling. The discussion ranged far and wide. Nevertheless, there was a certain euphoria in our talk. We sensed that there might be some historic significance in what we were about to do. Then I hit the somber note that toned us down. As best I can recall, I said something like this:

> The people who make up the Religious Right have something more than good organization, clever strategy, and a lot of money going for them. They have something more important in their favor. They have a couple of hot issues—issues that stir the emotions of people. They have issues that play on some of people's deepest concerns and most repressed fears.
>
> It is around these two issues that they have been able to build a unified movement. And you know what these issues are. I am talking about abortion rights and homosexual rights.

Before I could go any further, Marian Wright Edelman broke in with a simple declaration: "Yes! And what unifies them divides us."

We all fell silent for a long moment. Each of us cast our eyes about the room trying to take in the reactions of others. There was no doubt that we were facing up to a reality that could not be evaded. When the issues of homosexual rights and abortion rights are brought up, there is an immediate division in the ranks.

I looked over at Eugene Rivers, knowing full well that a good number of the black clergy, regardless of how much they worried about the onslaught of conservative political forces in America, were not about to join forces with any group that made gay and lesbian rights part of their agenda. For some hard-to-explain social and psychological reasons, the African American community, which itself has suffered enormous injustices at the hands of the dominant WASP society, often harbors prejudice against the gay and lesbian community that can easily translate into discriminatory social practices. Cornel West, professor of African American studies at Harvard, has carefully pointed out that homophobia is rampant in the black community and that most African Americans have not yet figured out that their liberation from social oppression is tied up with what happens to homosexual people and what happens to women.

I looked at Joe Hacala, a Franciscan brother. No matter how committed he might be to social justice in general, when it came to a woman's right to decide on the life and death of the unborn, there could be no compromise. We all knew that. In the constituency we were trying to put together, there would be many committed to a pro-choice stand on the abortion issue. On the other hand, we knew that with many of the progressives in the evangelical community, especially among the women in our ranks, there would be dissent against Joe's pro-life stance.

We stopped and prayed that God would help us discern what we should do and where we should go from there.

Chapter 8

The Hot Issues That Divide Us

The issues that divide my evangelical colleagues are issues that have divided the churches of my own denomination. They are issues that will not go away. On a more personal level, they are issues that divide my own family.

On the gay and lesbian issue, my wife, Peggy, is a member of an organization called Evangelicals Concerned, a group of Bible-believing Christians who argue that the Scriptures do not condemn monogamous marriages for homosexuals. Evangelicals Concerned contends that God allows for intimate committed relationships in which gay or lesbian partners can live out the kind of covenant that biblically prescribed marriage requires. In this, Peggy and I disagree. My wife and I belong to two different American Baptist churches. She belongs to a "welcoming and affirming church" that receives practicing homosexuals into membership. My church is like the overwhelming number of American Baptist churches that hold that same-gender sexual marriage is outside of any kind of lifestyle legitimated by Scripture.

Our argument comes down to a matter of hermeneutics. While there are other passages of Scripture that deal with homosexual activity, the one that ultimately divides us is Romans 1:26-28.

For this cause God gave them up unto vile affections: for even their women did change the natural use into that which is against nature: And likewise also the men, leaving the natural use of the woman, burned in their lust one toward another; men with men working that which is unseemly, and receiving in themselves that recompence of their error which was meet. And even as they did not like to retain God in their knowledge, God gave them over to a reprobate mind, to do those things which are not convenient.

Peggy argues that when Paul wrote this he was in the city of Corinth where the prevailing religion was the worship of Aphrodite. She notes that Aphrodite was a hermaphrodite with the sexual organs of both the male and female gender. In the worship of Aphrodite, people played the role of the opposite sex and engaged in sexual orgies with same-sex prostitutes who were available in the temple. These debauching orgies were an offense to Paul, and Peggy contends that it was against these orgies that he wrote in the first chapter of Romans. These orgies are condemned as filthy excesses that are the outcome of idolatry.

The context of Paul's condemnation of homosexual activity in this passage of Scripture, my wife believes, is an overall condemnation of idolatry and its consequences. And what Paul says here should not be applied to the kind of relationship that can be created between loving homosexual partners who are making a lifelong marital commitment. She claims that a careful reading of the entire first chapter of Romans will evidence an obvious connection between idolatry and homosexual practices.

In response to Peggy's argument, I contend that she is not only "stretching" the passage to bring it into agreement with her *a priori* beliefs, but she does so in the face of more than nineteen hundred years of church tradition. The church has been around for a long time, and never before have these verses been interpreted in this way. It is somewhat arrogant, I believe, to declare that nineteen hundred years of church tradition is wrong and that this brand-new interpretation of the first chapter of Romans is the correct one. Christian writings by the church fathers, some of whom knew Paul personally, clearly support the traditional condemnation of same-gender genital contact.

To my argument, Peggy responds with a reminder that nineteen hundred years of church tradition supported an interpretation of 1 Timothy 2:11 that disallowed women from church leadership and even from speaking in church. If we are willing to violate church traditions on the role of women, then why not do so for homosexuals? Maybe, she argues, nineteen hundred years of church tradition is wrong. After all, my wife says, "We're not Roman Catholics who put church tradition on the same level of authority as Scripture and consider it infallible."

But there is one other argument that I believe establishes my case. It is the argument "from nature." I believe that homosexuality is a condition that comes from being in a fallen world. It is not, in Kantian terms, "what ought to be."

All creatures, I believe, were created male and female for the purpose of procreation and for "replenishing the earth." Something went wrong as a consequence of the Adamic fall, and homosexuality is an expression of that.

This does not place any guilt on homosexuals for being who and what they are. We are all flawed by the Fall in one way or another. Homosexuals do not decide on their orientation any more than heterosexuals do. But, while they do not choose what they are, they do decide what they are going to do. And the Bible has directives as to what Christians can and cannot do if they are to be faithful to God's will for their lives.

The empirical evidence lends support to my argument. In in-depth interviews I have had with more than three hundred gay men, I found that all of them had wanted to change. There was a general sadness among them that they could not enjoy what they deemed to be a natural life that included getting into the kind of marriage that gives birth to children. Peggy argues that homosexuals feel this way because society has made them feel this way. But I believe that the homosexual orientation is contrary to what is normative in nature and that it runs counter to what naturally ensures the survival of the human species. Needless to say, there are some very interesting (but loving) arguments and discussions around our house.

There are those who argue that I ought not to "allow" my wife to go around the country "spouting off" her views when they are contrary to mine. One prominent televangelist has claimed that since I do not have my wife "in submission" in this matter, I have forfeited my right to preach the gospel.

This opinion is especially prevalent among those who take Paul's admonition in Ephesians 5:24 to mean that a man should not allow his wife to have opinions different from his own. Paul writes: "Therefore as the church is subject unto Christ, so let the wives be to their own husbands in every thing."

To those who think that obeying Paul's admonition means that I should not allow my wife to express opinions different from mine, I have two responses. First, I suggest that Peggy and I are modeling what Christian marriage is all about. Ours is a marriage in which we respect each other's opinions and defend each other's right to be a person with his or her own ideas and beliefs.

I contend that when Paul speaks about submission, he is not providing grounds for male domination, nor is he calling for a wife to suppress her thinking in such a way as to deny her humanity. Paul talks about *mutual* submission in Ephesians 5:21. Wives, indeed, are supposed to submit to their husbands. But the same passage declares that in response, husbands are supposed to love their wives "as Christ also loved the church, and gave himself for it" (v. 25). Clearly, in Philippians 2:5-11, Paul makes it clear that Christ's love for the church made him willing to be a servant. Actually the word *dulos* in the original language of the New Testament, which is translated as "servant" in the King James Version, would be better translated as "slave." If men are to love their wives as Christ loved the church, the *dulos* style would hardly fit with the kind of domination that my critics suggest I exercise over Peggy.

If there is anything that is clear to me in Scripture, it is that those socially prescribed roles for males and females that tyrannize the personhood of either have been obliterated through Christ's ministry on the cross. The concept of the inferiority of women has been overcome because of what he did there. "There is neither Jew nor Greek, there is neither bond nor free, there is neither male nor female: for ye are all one in Christ Jesus" (Galatians 3:28).

The oneness here declared does away with hierarchy and establishes a new basis for equality and mutual respect. The leadership of a husband in a Christian marriage is no longer a patriarchal kind of domination that crushes a woman's individuality. There is instead a "servant" leadership that empowers the wife to express herself and realize her unique individuality.

Second, I believe that what is going on between Peggy and me, as we differ from each other on this crucial culture-war issue, is modeling in a personal way what the church needs to embrace—the fact that serious differences do not necessitate a divorce. The tension of our disagreements is actually a polar tension that holds us together. Dialogue is what relationships are all about at their best, and if Peggy and I agreed on everything, there would not be a need for one of us.

On many issues, Christians must learn that on this side of glory *there may not be resolutions* to those dramatically opposed beliefs that divide us. We must learn to live in unity while affirming our individual right to differ. This is at the heart of the Baptist tradition.

The Causes of Homosexuality

The truth is that nobody knows what causes a homosexual orientation. We have heard the various theories that oversimplify it all. Some attribute homosexuality to sociological conditioning, such as inadequate identification with the parent of the same or opposite sex. Others believe they can trace the cause to genetic factors that affect such things as the development of the hypothalamus gland, which controls sexual behavior. There are still other theories that see biophysical conditions *in utero* as predisposing the unborn to a tendency toward a homosexual orientation.

But those whom I believe to be the experts in the field of study that deals with homosexuality contend that there is probably a multiplicity of factors that come together to establish the effect. What complicates things more, they argue, is that these factors interact in different ways and to different degrees in different individuals. All of this leads me to the obvious conclusion that those "easy-to-understand" explanations of homosexuality that are heard on religious radio talk shows are oversimplifications that simply are not true.

Perhaps of more serious consequence is the fact that there is no simple way out of a homosexual orientation. Those who suggest that there are some "surefire" counseling techniques guaranteed to change a person's sexual orientation are probably offering false hope to those who would like to change. Sadly, I have to say that not even religious conversion offers a ready solution for the homosexual who wants to be "straight." So many homosexuals who have sought change through religious means have ended up not only disillusioned but convinced that somehow God despises them in a special way. They have heard from the pulpit that God regards homosexuals as a special abomination, and that if they would get right with God they would be free from homosexual temptation. After giving themselves over to God in every way that they can, pleading in agony for God to change them, they are left to conclude that they have been predestined for damnation. The spiritual and psychological despair that follows is often more than they can bear. Suicide is now the second major cause of death among teenagers and, according to one report, one-third of those suicides are committed by youngsters who despise themselves because of their sexual orientation.

I don't know everything that the church should be about these days, but we certainly should not be about creating the despair that leads to self-destruction.

I am not saying that God cannot change people from being homosexuals into being heterosexuals. *God can do anything!* I am only saying that empirically we find that the overwhelming number of those who have sought "deliverance" through faith commitments have found that after all is said and done, nothing has changed.

Some of my evangelical friends refuse even to consider the empirical evidence. They want to believe that if homosexuals just repent and seek counseling, all will be well. They just don't get it. People can repent of what they do, but they cannot repent of who they are. Being homosexual is not just a bad habit that can be broken. It is an essential part of the identity of some of our brothers and sisters. Those who refuse the empirical evidence often do so in the belief that homosexuals actually decide to be homosexual or are "messed up" because they were molested as children. Such conclusions allow them to believe that all homosexuals can be changed and therefore are "guilty" if they accept their homosexual orientation, rather than becoming involved in some kind of spiritually therapeutic cure process. If these people would only talk to enough homosexuals over extended periods of time, they would realize how hard most of them have tried and prayed and sought counseling—to no avail.

A Good Way to Help Gays and Lesbians

What I hope for is more understanding for homosexuals from the rest of the Christian community. I want gays and lesbians to find in the church fellow Christians ready to support them as they come to terms with their sexual orientation and struggle daily to overcome the temptations that they must face.

Personally, I look forward to a time when the church will

have learned to respond to homosexuals in the same way that we respond to alcoholics. My wife does not like me making this comparison because it implies that homosexuality is a sickness. She has a point; but for the sake of my argument, allow me to continue in this line of thought.

There was a time when we assumed that alcoholism could be overcome simply by religious conversion. We expected alcoholics to be able to stand up at testimony meetings in church and say something like this: "I was once an alcoholic. But then Jesus saved me, and since that day I have never had any desire for drink. The Lord took away all my craving for that cursed brew, and now I am completely free."

Undoubtedly, there are a few people who *can* give testimonies just like this. As a matter of fact, Glen Campbell, the well-known popular singer, claims such a miraculous healing and has told his story often on network television talk shows. However, what is far more often the case is that the alcoholic who wants to stay sober is in for a daily struggle against temptation for the rest of his or her life. Nowadays a converted alcoholic in a supportive Christian community usually has a testimony that goes something like this:

I *am* an alcoholic! I haven't had anything to drink for a long while. But the desire for drink is always with me, and I have to win the struggle against the temptation one day at a time. I want you to know that I am not alone in my struggle. I depend on a Higher Power, and there are also brothers and sisters who pray for me and are there for me in my times of dire need. Without them to support me, I would never make it. This is not a struggle that anyone can win on his or her own.

In parallel fashion, I am hoping that someday the church will allow a person who is homosexual to say:

I *am* a homosexual! I have not committed the kind of homosexual acts that the Bible forbids since I gave my life to Christ. But every day I have to fight the battle against temptation over again. I want to thank God for the strength that he gives me in this daily struggle, and I also thank God for the help of Christian friends. If it were not for my Christian brothers and sisters praying for me and upholding me, I wouldn't be able to make it.

The people of God should be able to offer this kind of support to gays and lesbians who are part of their church fellowship. We are admonished to "bear one another's burdens" in order to "so fulfil the law of Christ" (Galatians 6:2).

Conversion to Christ and membership in the body does not mean that a person will not experience temptation any more. It only means that, with the help of the Lord and the strength derived from Christian fellowship, he or she can be "more than a conqueror" (Romans 8:37).

Right now we are a far cry from any sympathetic undergirding of homosexual Christians who have chosen to be celibate out of devotion to Christ. The reality is that the evangelical community is, for the most part, opposed to any such suggestion of sympathy. When President Clinton tried to change things so that homosexuals in the military would not have to conceal their sexual identity in order to remain in good standing, there was an outcry in most evangelical churches. They wanted no part of a system wherein gays and lesbians could tell the truth about who they were and still remain in uniform. And yet, without that truth, there can be little hope and few victories.

I really don't know what we evangelicals think we have to gain by forcing gays and lesbians in the military to conceal their identity. There is no question that they are already there. Estimates of the number of homosexuals in the military exceed twenty thousand. Do we Christians want these hurting people to have to lie to evade court martial? And if we want to win them to Christ, do we not have to create a social environment in which they can be honest about who they are?

We cannot have the kind of meaningful dialogue that leads to conversion unless those we witness to can be open to us and allow themselves to be vulnerable. When gays and lesbians have to conceal their true identities to keep their commissions in the military, hold jobs in the school system, and escape residential discrimination, it is not possible to minister to their real needs.

These are realities that all evangelicals, including those in the American Baptist Churches, will have to think through if they are to escape the label of homophobia, which is all too often applied to them. The day of simple answers to the complex problems surrounding homosexuality is gone forever. All evangelicals must ask themselves if they have realistic Good News for gays and lesbians who want to follow the Lord and be members of their churches.

The Hottest Issue in the Culture Wars

There is another problem that has evangelicals in an uproar and has made them easy prey for those who would persuade or pressure them to join the Religious Right. This is the controversy surrounding the abortion issue.

It has been pointed out by many people, notable among them Carl Henry, former professor and dean at Eastern Baptist Theological Seminary, that evangelicals have a history of being so committed to winning individuals to Christ that they have ignored the biblical requisites to work for social justice. Up until the 1950s, most evangelicals shied away from any social action initiatives, believing that social action programs were a distraction of liberals. Liberals, they said, wanted us to get into their Social Gospel rather than getting on with the task of winning people to Christ.

But all of that changed with the *Roe* v. *Wade* decision by the Supreme Court. Suddenly, the sleeping giant of the body of born-again believers was awakened to the need to get politically involved. The abortion issue got them into high gear, and since that time evangelicals have organized and reorganized themselves politically. Recently, they have done so with increasing sophistication and effectiveness.

The abortion issue has been one of the banners around

which evangelicals have rallied to exercise their demands for change in America. Without the abortion issue, movements like the Christian Coalition would probably have far less viability today.

Ron Sider, the founder and executive director of Evangelicals for Social Action, has made abortion one of the issues on which ESA has made a clear and definitive stand. Its strong and unequivocal pro-life stand may have kept many evangelical feminists from joining this now predominantly male organization. Nevertheless, members of this most recognizable of moderate-to-left groups hold tenaciously to what they believe to be a stand that cannot be compromised.

The Religious Right, however, has done much better than ESA or any other such moderate group in making the pro-life crusade a banner for its cause. Consequently, the Religious Right has gained much support within the evangelical wing of almost every mainline denomination. It is the allegiance of such pro-lifers within the American Baptist Churches that poses a serious problem for the leaders of this denomination. These leaders are trying to maintain a course that, on a variety of social issues, is much more liberal than that taken by the Religious Right. But they find themselves without credibility with evangelical pro-life American Baptists.

There was a time when most mainline denominations, American Baptist Churches included, had resolutions on record that defined them as being fairly liberal on the issue of abortion. In December of 1981, the General Board of the American Baptist Churches voted the following:

> We recognize that the First Amendment guarantee of the free exercise of religion protects the right of a person, in consultation with her advisor, spiritual counselor and physician, to make a decision of conscience for or against an abortion. We call for every action which will ensure full preservation of this First Amendment freedom.

For all intents and purposes, this resolution lent support to the pro-choice position that whether or not to have an abortion is a decision that belongs to the individual. This stirred to action the politically conservative wing of the American Baptist Churches, which usually paid little attention to the resolutions passed at the conventions of their denomination. First at meetings on the state level and then at national meetings, pro-life evangelicals made impassioned pleas for the rescuing of the unborn. No longer were they indifferent to denominational gatherings. Instead, such gatherings became an important battleground for fighting it out with their adversaries in the culture wars.

This issue was especially upsetting for American Baptists because our denomination, more than any other, has a constituency with a wide diversity. Consider the fact that Carl Henry, the dean of American evangelicalism, and Harvey Cox, the liberal Harvard religion professor, both claim membership in American Baptist churches.

American Baptists and Abortion

American Baptists have had a long tradition of Christian feminism, and the concerns of feminists have heightened the intensity of the abortion debate. Over the last few decades, many Christian feminists have argued for the right of women to make those decisions that determine their biological destiny. With other feminists, American Baptists in this movement have argued that a woman's body is her own, and that no ecclesiastical organization (especially not one dominated by male leaders) has the right to determine what will be allowed to happen to it.

The counterargument has been that when dealing with abortion, the issue is not a matter of a woman deciding what will happen to *her* body. Instead, the pregnant woman considering an abortion is deciding what will happen to the body of an unborn child. No one, contend pro-life evangelicals, has the right to deny another human being the right to life.

The opposition to abortion has become increasingly intense in recent years, and the leaders of the American Baptist

Churches, realizing that the debate has all the ingredients that could lead to a major schism, have reexamined their denomination's stand on the issue. They sponsored a number of conferences and hearings that led to a restatement in 1988 of the American Baptist position, which reads in part:

> As American Baptists we oppose abortion
>   as a means of avoiding responsibility for conception,
>   as a primary means of birth control,
>   without regard for the far-reaching consequences of the act.

This revised statement, while not categorically pro-life, certainly was a move away from support of the clearly pro-choice position passed in 1981, which made abortion solely a matter of individual conscience. Nevertheless, this matter is by no means settled. What pro-life supporters expect from their denomination is a definitive condemnation of abortion along with a commitment to lobby those in government to pass the legislation that will make it illegal.

What makes the abortion issue particularly difficult for denominational leaders is the fact that there are few clear-cut biblical references that deal directly with the issue. Those who are strongly pro-life say that, in the final analysis, the commandment set down by God, "Thou shalt not kill" should be enough. The problem is that pro-choice proponents argue that this verse refers specifically to killing human beings, and they believe that there is little basis for establishing that the fetus *is* a human being.

The pro-life people counter with verses such as these:

> Did not he that made me in the womb make him? and did not one fashion us in the womb? (Job 31:15).

> For thou hast possessed my reins: thou hast covered me in my mother's womb. I will praise thee; for I am fearfully and wonderfully made: marvellous are thy works; and that my soul knoweth right well. My substance was not hid from thee, when I was made in secret, and curiously wrought in the lowest parts of the earth. Thine eyes did see my substance, yet being unperfect; and in thy book all my members

were written, which in continuance were fashioned, when as yet there was none of them (Psalm 139:13-16).

These and other verses, they argue, suggest that God has defined the unborn as persons with spiritual characteristics. Being known by God as persons is sufficient, they say, to establish the humanness of the unborn child.

"Not so!" respond the pro-choicers, who will be satisfied with nothing less than some specific and clear biblical reference that reads like: "Thou shalt not abort the unborn."

The pro-choice argument rests on the assumption that the unborn fetus has not yet been humanized. I have heard a number of justifications of this assumption, but the one that makes the most sense to me is that the "humanness" of a person is imparted through a relational process. Only the experiencing of empathetic rapport with another can bring about humanization. Humanness, according to this argument, is not so much biological inheritance as it is a social interactive process. The pro-choice people say that during the first eight to ten weeks of embryonic development, before the developing fetus has an operative brain, there is no possibility for the kind of interaction between mother and child that would initiate humanization. Thus, abortion should be permissible during this early period.

It is further argued by pro-choice advocates that if it were possible to bring an infant *Homo sapiens* into the world without any meaningful relationships with humans, then the traits of humanness would never develop in that *Homo sapiens*. Such a child, like one raised by wolves, would have only the traits and characteristics of the creatures that raised it. Such a child, it is contended, would have no language, no concept of morality, no concept of God, and no reflective consciousness of being human. Socialization, so this argument goes, is the means through which a *Homo sapiens* becomes human.

While this theory has some logic in its favor, there is one flaw. That is that there is increasing evidence that the process of social interaction begins *before* birth. The mother carrying a baby interacts with that unborn child in a variety

of meaningful ways, all of which are not yet clear to re-
searchers. If we are to deem the child "human" from the point
at which humanizing socialization begins, we will have to
give serious attention to what these influences are and how
early *in utero* the humanization process begins.

The argument over abortion, as you might surmise, will
probably go on and on without resolution. And this is what
makes the problem so difficult for those who have to govern
a mainline denomination like the American Baptist
Churches. It is a divisive issue, and those on both sides are
intensely committed to making their respective positions the
official stance of the denomination.

In reality, many Christians remain uncertain on the issue.
Many remain unconvinced by either the ardent pro-life or
pro-choice advocates. Neither side has effectively dialogued
with this uncommitted group. These confused, undecided
Christians have been confronted by protest marches and
increasingly strained confrontations with the advocates of
both sides, but there has been little light shed on the issue to
help them make up their minds.

This is an argument in which pro-choice and pro-life people
agree on only one thing: there *is* no middle ground. But the
middle ground is where most Americans, and more specifically, most church members, stand on this issue. In his book
The Battle Over the Family, Peter Berger, a prominent Lutheran sociologist, makes this point effectively.

Berger suggests that most people who consider themselves
pro-choice would object strenuously to permitting abortions
in the last month of pregnancy, or for that matter in the last
three months of a pregnancy. On the other hand, he contends,
a significant proportion of those who call themselves pro-life
would reluctantly accept abortions in the earliest stages of
pregnancy, especially in cases that involve rape or incest. We
would find, says Berger, that among many pro-life Christians
there is acceptance of the "morning-after" pills that have
been developed in France. Many people in the church, he
contends, are not strongly pro-life or pro-choice. We would

find that there is a silent group that is confused, but does not want to discuss the issue because they are afraid of the heated argument that would follow.

Berger also claims that many Christians change their opinions on the abortion issue when faced with personal situations in which undesirable pregnancies become problematic. To support his claim, one survey shows that 20 percent of abortions are performed on women who claim to be committed evangelical Christians and who, on the ideological level, believe abortion to be wrong. As a case in support of this point, I have a friend who took a very conservative stance on this issue until his daughter had an unwanted pregnancy outside of a marital relationship. Then suddenly, he became a pro-choice supporter.

When all the pros and cons on this issue have been heard, it can be argued that it might be safest to adopt a pro-life position. Many moderates argue that, since the issue cannot be conclusively decided in either a scientific manner or through Scripture, it is best to chance making an error on the side of life. After all, they say, if one takes a pro-choice position and it is wrong, one will have lent support to the killing of innocent children. Furthermore, these moderates argue, all life should be treated as sacred, whether or not it can be determined that, in the case of abortion, we are dealing with *human* life. These moderates are repulsed by the way in which abortion has come to be treated so casually that it has simply become another form of birth control. But there are women who respond to such logic by saying, "This is the kind of thing we expected to hear from men who do not personally know what an unwanted pregnancy is all about."

There is much to suggest that, in the end, the American Baptist Churches, along with most other mainline denominations, may turn away from strong pro-choice sympathies in order to gain the support of the pro-life evangelicals. "Institutional considerations," as they say, may win out in the minds of denominational leaders who realize how necessary it is to keep evangelicals in the fold. And there will be ardent feminists who will say, "You just can't trust male leaders to stand up for us."

Personally, I think waffling on crucial issues is not the way to go. I think that integrity demands that people be true to their convictions and not make adaptations of their beliefs just for "institutional considerations." Support for denominational churches cannot be won at the expense of people compromising what they believe to be true.

As the stresses and strains of the culture wars threaten the precarious unity of mainline denominations, there are circumstances that have made things different from ever before. As I have said, a survey of the recent history of American denominational life will show that the executive leadership of denominations was always somewhat to the theological and political left of their constituency. Consequently, the churches that were disgruntled and prone to separating from denominational membership were usually the more conservative churches. As modernism swept through Protestantism during the early part of this century, the schismatic tendencies were always from the fundamentalists.

Denominational leaders had a sufficient power base among liberal churches to resist the demands of these fundamentalists. In the end, it was those churches and clergy whose conservative beliefs and practices were not expressed in denominational programs that usually withdrew their affiliation. It was always the fundamentalists who established either independent churches or new and separate denominations. Certainly these were the circumstances that led to the split-offs from the American Baptist Churches, U.S.A. that became the General Assembly of Regular Baptists and the Conservative Baptist Association.

What makes things so different these days is that now the dissident churches tend to be to the theological and political left of the mainstream of mainline denominations. They are also to the left of most denominational executives. The problem facing most mainline denominations is whether or not they will be able to hold their more liberal and radical churches within the denominational ranks. It is now the more liberal churches that are on the fringe of denominational life.

As a case in point, my wife's church, which welcomes into membership gays and lesbians who are in same-sex committed relationships, even performs commitment services that bless homosexual marriages. Whereas such avant-garde practices would have been tolerated in the past, in today's milieu, this church becomes a major embarrassment for the denominational leaders. There is even some talk of putting such churches out of the denomination's fellowship.

What has changed is that there has been a power shift in the nation. Conservatism has been making a dramatic comeback. This is evident not only in the politics in Washington but also in the politics at the headquarters of mainline denominations. Whereas conservatives in the past were usually diffused voices crying in the wilderness, they have, as of late, learned how to create unified organizational power blocs that can lobby their points of view into policy.

The power these days is with those churches on the theological and political right of denominational executives, and the executives know it. They are more likely to make concessions to the demands of conservatives than to yield to the demands of the more liberal members and churches in their denomination's membership. It is no longer chic for denominational leaders to be liberal. It is dangerous!

A prominent Presbyterian minister I recently interviewed told me that he would not be surprised if the liberal congregations in the Presbyterian Church (USA) that espoused homosexual marriages and pro-choice positions on abortion eventually withdrew from his denomination and joined the Metropolitan Churches of America. This is a new denomination that was created by homosexuals who wanted churches that embraced their lifestyle. What he predicted about the liberal churches of his own denomination may also be what the future holds for the liberal churches of other denominations.

The tide has turned against liberalism in the society at

large, and this changing tide is being felt by the mainline denominations as well.

There is a better way to handle such conflicts, but it will require more than some good diplomacy by denominational leaders. It will require a whole restructuring of how denominations work. We are talking here of a new system of organizing churches within mainline denominations so that people can hold to their convictions within churches of like-minded people, while still participating with churches that have members with contradictory views. It can be done, but not without some dramatic changes that will be hard for many to accept.

The rest of this book is designed to spell out ways that mainline denominations can make a comeback. The first matter to be addressed has to be the matter of restructuring.

Part II

Prescriptions

Introduction

On the Comeback Trail

Mainline denominations did not lose members during the last three decades because people gave up on religion. What really happened was what sociologists call "cultural lag." Mainline church members found their churches' religious and social values becoming more and more out of touch with their own ways of thinking. The people in the pews grew impatient with churches stuck in forms of worship that seemed to belong to another era. They often considered denominational programs to be the creations of theological eggheads unaware of the constituents' wants and needs.

The people who left mainline denominations were, for the most part, looking for something altogether different from what was being offered to them in their churches. But they were not turning away from Christianity. On the contrary, the stresses and strains of their increasingly difficult and complicated lives made them seek out biblical answers to their problems. They simply did not find what they were looking for in mainline churches. Certainly some gave up on Christianity. But millions of others, desperate for a relevant expression of their faith, turned to the new breed of nondenominational evangelical churches that seemed to be springing up everywhere.

For mainline churches to make a comeback, they must pick up on the positive developments of modern evangelicalism, incorporating into their own ministries whatever works best. Those changes, combined with an escape from the political agenda of the Religious Right, could very well transform old, denominational churches into strong, vital congregations attracting hosts of new members.

Great numbers of people are looking for a relevant, biblically sound gospel that does not force them into the politics of groups like the Christian Coalition. These people want forms of worship that are engaging and contemporary but that are still linked to the historic Christian traditions that gave birth to mainline denominations. These people crave a transforming personal relationship with the resurrected Christ, but also want to be part of a community of believers committed to liberating the poor, saving the environment, and creating a just social order for everyone, including people of color, women, and homosexuals. These people appreciate the emphasis on personal salvation so central to evangelicalism, but also appreciate the progressive social agenda promoted by traditional denominational churches.

The time is ripe for a renewal of mainline denominations, but the time is short as well. There are changes that must be made quickly, and some of those changes are difficult to face—especially for denominational leaders who see them as threatening.

While almost everyone concerned about the renewal and growth of mainline denominational churches agrees that radical changes are desperately needed, there are major debates over just what those changes should be. What follows is my perspective.

On the one hand, from my own observations and discussions with hundreds of church leaders, from both the evangelical community and the mainline denominations, I am fairly convinced that these proposals are on target. On the other hand, I expect them to elicit justifiable criticisms and corrections. Whether or not these are the best solutions, the fact is that they address the fundamental problems facing all mainline denominations. More than anything, I hope that what I say contributes to an intense and immediate discussion of those issues that must be dealt with if mainline denominational churches are to become a dynamic and viable presence in the twenty-first century.

I will first list the changes I believe are most essential and then go on to explain how these changes can be brought about in my own denomination, American Baptist Churches in the U.S.A. Fortunately, the polity of our denomination makes it an ideal candidate for the changes I propose. Other denominations may find that their governing rules and regulations make such changes much more difficult to implement. Nevertheless, I believe my suggestions can be, and should be, implemented by all of the mainline denominations. Few things would please me more than the American Baptist Churches becoming the leaders, blazing a comeback trail that other denominations could quickly follow.

At the core of my conclusions is a belief that mainline denominations will survive only if their leaders realize that the time is past for them to function as programming bureaucracies. Over and over again, I will try to drive home the point that in all sectors of our society there is a shifting of power and planning to the local level. Central to all that I am about to lay out for your consideration is a belief that the local church must once again become the primary agent for theological reflection, program planning, and missionary enterprises. Denominations have a future only as support agents for local church ministries.

There was a time when local churches may have been viewed as instruments for carrying out the grand schemes for ministry to the world that were hatched in denominational headquarters. But in the future, denominations will have to restructure themselves so that they assume the more humble role of helpmates to empower local congregations to think through, plan, and execute ministries that those congregations define as relevant. This may take more grace than most of those who have a vested interest in preserving the old bureaucracies can muster.

Now comes the hard part. In the rest of this book, I will make eight increasingly radical proposals which I believe to be the comeback trail for mainline denominations. While I am confident that I am on the right track, many who read my proposals may find themselves wondering, "Is this guy serious?"

I assure you, I am.

Recruiting the Finest and the Best for Church Leadership

Every study that has been made to analyze what makes churches grow points to the same thing—the quality and effectiveness of pastoral leadership. To make a comeback, mainline denominations simply must recruit and train a more effective clergy. This is particularly true of American Baptist Churches in the U.S.A. Obviously, we are not getting the best and brightest of our people to become pastors. I do not mean to put down in any way those talented ABC pastors who have mastered their vocation and made their churches grow according to their biblical mandates. But I do declare that we are letting the vast majority of our most gifted young people get away without ever having challenged them to seriously consider pastoral ministry as a great and noble vocation.

For the most part, the way we get our pastors is when they present themselves to us, announcing that they have been called into the ministry. We are usually so pleased with their desire to go into "full-time Christian service" that we are not about to question their calling or ask if they have the gifts that being an effective pastor requires.

When confronted by someone who tells us that he or she has been called to ministry, we usually feel somewhat intimidated. We might have some doubts about the character or capacities of this particular candidate for ministry, but we generally show little inclination to raise any of the crucial questions that should be raised about those who aspire to pastoral positions. We feel especially reluctant to raise questions if the would-be pastor shows evidence of the fruit of the Spirit: love, joy, peace, longsuffering, gentleness, goodness, faith, meekness, temperance (Galatians 5:22-23).

While the spiritual quality of a person has great importance in determining whether he or she qualifies for Christian ministry, most of us realize that spirituality alone does not make someone an effective leader of a congregation. Our churches need good preachers. We need people who can communicate the gospel message in ways that are both intelligible and interesting.

We do not have to encourage a cultic appreciation of preachers to recognize that without powerful messengers in the pulpits, the message usually is not heard. We may decry the fact that television has conditioned our people to expect that the gospel be presented in an exciting, entertaining fashion, but the fact remains that it has. So now, more than ever, we need to call into the ministry persons who not only have the fruit of the Spirit, but who also possess the essential gifts of the Spirit—the gift of preaching in this case. If we are going to bring people into our churches and incorporate them into our ministries, we have to recognize the need for pastors who can hold people's attention when they stand up to speak on Sunday mornings. Before we affirm someone's calling into the pastoral ministry, we should have some evidence or demonstration that God has given this person the gift of preaching. If there is no consensus in the church that the candidate has those gifts, there should be a gentle questioning as to whether or not this calling is from God or stems from some other motivation.

There are too many who get into ministry out of guilt or to please a parent. There are too many people who find themselves preaching behind the sacred desk because of attempts to compensate for some psychological dysfunction or some feeling of moral inadequacy.

For instance, the pastorate has a great attraction for those who have exhibitionist tendencies. There are all too many who go into the ministry out of the psychological need to gain public recognition rather than out of love for the Lord. Do not get me wrong. I am convinced that good preachers have to have some of the theatrical in their personalities to be good at their craft. But the need to draw attention to self can be exaggerated to unhealthy levels.

A friend of mine had this point illustrated to him once by an elderly woman in a church he visited. Following the morning worship service, the pastor's son ran up on the platform and into the pulpit. The microphone was still on, so everyone lingering in the sanctuary was jerked to attention as the little boy yelled over the P.A. system, "Look everybody! I'm in the pulpit!"

The elderly woman muttered to my friend, "That's his father's message every Sunday."

There are others who make the pulpit into an instrument for expressing their repressed angers. The story is told of a deacon who told his neighbor about the new preacher in town. "He's okay," the older man said with a sigh, "but he's not as good as the last one we had."

"What was the last one like?" asked the neighbor.

The deacon answered, "Oh, the last one told us we're all sinners, and that if we don't repent we'll suffer in hell."

"And what does the new preacher of yours say?"

"Well, this one also tells us that we're all sinners and that if we don't repent we'll all suffer in hell."

"Then what's the difference?" asked the neighbor.

"This new one doesn't say it with tears in his eyes."

Sometimes those in the pulpit are working out their own hostilities as they thunder God's judgment on their people.

In many cases there are people whose lives become disasters and who wreck the churches that they try to serve, all because no one had the courage to raise the right questions when these pastors first declared that they felt "called." On a latent level, the doubts about the would-be pastors were commonly felt, but no one came out and said that they failed to see the traits of a good preacher evident in the candidate. However, when these candidates move on to pastorates and then fail horribly, these same church folk openly confess, "I'm not surprised. I never did think he/she should have been a preacher in the first place."

The problem becomes even more pronounced if the troubled ministerial candidate is a woman. The examination committee, especially if it is made up of men who are afraid of seeming to be sexist or chauvinistic, are likely to leave the candidate's personal qualities for ministry unquestioned. This, of course, is a good reason to ensure that any pulpit committee is composed half and half of men and women. In this day of transition to the acceptance of women into the ministry, we must not be intimidated into accepting candidates just on the basis of gender.

Challenge the Talented

I am suggesting that we examine the Scriptures and take another look at the process used by first-century Christians for selecting their pastoral leaders and preachers. In the New Testament, the church did not let individuals declare themselves "called"! Instead, the people of God together determined who in their midst had the gift of God for preaching. When someone in the church demonstrated that he or she had the communication skills and the "people skills" that it took to be an effective pastor, the church was *proactive*. The church people held prayer sessions so they could get some confirmation from the Lord. And when the key leaders of the church were in unanimous agreement, they called that person who they sensed had the gifts required to be an outstanding minister and presented that person with the challenge to become a pastor.

We are far too individualistic in our concept of establishing calls into the ministry. The early church would not accept as a pastor someone who told them that he or she was "called." Quite the opposite! Instead, it was the church that did the calling. The Bible says, particularly in the book of Acts, that the church set aside those deemed to possess the character and the gifts that would make them effective preachers and missionaries (Acts 6:3-4 and 11:22).

The life of George W. Truett, whom many consider to be the greatest Baptist preacher in the last hundred years, certainly follows this pattern. Truett was a lawyer in Dallas, Texas, and a member of the First Baptist Church. He actually served on the pulpit committee that was seeking a new pastor to lead that church. In the process of reviewing candidates, there arose a general agreement among the other members of the pulpit committee (and later among the entire congregation) that Truett himself had the gifts to be the kind of pastor they needed.

At a rather dramatic meeting, the congregation confronted Truett and informed him of their unified conviction that he should be their pastor. Truett at first protested and declared that they had no right to tell him what to do with his life and that they certainly had no right to demand that he be their pastor. But the congregation persisted and said in no uncertain terms that since they were all in agreement and that he was the only one in disagreement, then in all probability he was not in harmony with the will of God. They explained that it was not likely that he alone could discern the will of God more accurately than a whole congregation at prayer.

Truett's protests were to no avail, and in the end, he capitulated to the collective will of the body of Christ. The consequences were spectacular. George W. Truett went on to become one of the best preachers and most effective pastors that Baptists in America have ever known.

All of this is to make the point that we are not going about getting people into the pastoral ministry in either the most effective or the most biblical manner.

Individualism, that most sacred value of Western culture,

is a Christian heresy. To be fully Christian, according to the Scriptures, the individual must submit to the authority of the body of Christ (1 Corinthians 12). Even if a person believes that he or she has heard the voice of God giving orders to become a preacher, that person still must be subject to the church for confirmation that the calling did, indeed, come from God. That process, of course, is one way that the early church escaped from having as pastors psychotics who *thought* they had heard the Word of the Lord. How I wish the church exercised such care today.

There is one more thing that I believe should be added to this proposal about calling the right people to the ministry: that is the responsibility that a church has to undergird those who are recognized by the church to be pastors and preachers.

When the pastor died at my own church, the Mount Carmel Baptist Church of West Philadelphia, the pulpit committee selected to succeed him a young man who was just graduating from the theological seminary. Being told of the youth and seeming inexperience of the candidate, I told the chairperson of the committee, "We shouldn't be taking a young man just out of seminary and making him the pastor of a two-thousand-member church. We ought to go out and get ourselves one of the great preachers of our denomination to take this pulpit."

One old deacon shot back at me, "Tony, we're going to take this young preacher, and we're going to *make* him one of the great preachers of this denomination."

Over the years that followed, I watched our church do exactly that. The support, love, and encouragement that they gave our pastor made him into one of the very finest preachers in this nation.

Congregations must seriously consider the role that they play in developing preachers who are effective communicators. I have seen congregations that have built up the confidence of their pastors and encouraged them to greatness. But far too often, I have seen congregations destroy young preachers and drive them not only out of the pastorate, but out of any kind of relationship with the church. If mainline denominations are going to make a comeback, they have to teach the people in the pews that they play a major role in making the pastors that serve them into great preachers and leaders. And as I stated earlier, whether or not churches have outstanding leadership is the most decisive factor in determining the success or failure of those churches.

In all of this discussion about what we should look for in candidates for the pastorate, I want to emphasize that, above all, those who would lead our churches must be men and women of deep spiritual commitment. More often than any of us are willing to admit, the pastorate is viewed as a "cushy" job that attracts the lazy rather than the godly. Realistically, the pastoral ministry is a job that is usually designed by the person who does it. Some pastors design their jobs so that they become workaholics who never stop. But there are others who do little but pass the time from Sunday to Sunday. Only the properly spiritual pastor can manage to live a balanced life, bringing to the task an earnestness and commitment that will increasingly model the lifestyle of our Lord.

Sören Kierkegaard observed that it is one thing for a man to so love people with God's love that he would give his life on a cross to save them. It is quite another thing, said Kierkegaard, for someone to expect to earn a good salary for once a week *describing* a man who gave his life on a cross.

We need "Type A" personalities with entrepreneurial risk-taking attributes in our pulpits. But more importantly, they must be balanced people who are constrained to serve because of their spirituality and love.

Redesigning Seminary Education

The spiritual renewal and growth of mainline denominations not only requires that we recruit the right people into pastoral leadership; it also requires that we properly prepare them for service. At this point, I have to raise some serious questions about our seminaries.

First of all, we simply have too many of them. In the case of American Baptists, there are four seminaries that are exclusively ours (Eastern, Northern, Central, and the American Baptist Seminary of the West) and five that we share with other denominations, of which I make recommendations about only two (Andover Newton and Colgate Rochester/Bexley Hall/Crozer)[1]. All of them are struggling, chronically in need of more students and more money.

I believe it would be best to merge some of these schools in order to create one absolutely first-rate training institution. Specifically, Eastern, Northern, and Central seminaries could be easily combined. They represent very similar theological traditions and share very similar visions of church ministry. Such a merger would yield a bigger, better seminary *and* save a whole lot of money.

It made sense to have separate schools back in the days when air travel was either difficult and expensive or nonex-

nation to provide ready access for students and a ready
supply of ministers to meet regional needs. But times have
changed. Now that the nation can be crossed relatively inex-
pensively and in a matter of hours by airplane, there is no
reason why one "superschool" could not adequately serve
the entire denomination. For American Baptists to provide
the kind of theological education that they want their pastors
to have, they must consolidate their resources and put together the kind of world-class faculty, staff, and programs
that none of their present schools could possibly manage.

We may well ask whether or not the American Baptist
Seminary of the West really has any reason to continue. It
has few students and seems somewhat unattractive even to
those candidates for ministry who come from California.
Already, Fuller Theological Seminary in Pasadena consistently has more American Baptists in its student body and
has achieved such high academic standards that, at this
point, our best move might be to simply shut down the
American Baptist Seminary of the West, invest those resources in my proposed national seminary, and simply direct
seminarians who want to stay on the West Coast to study at
Fuller. I know this idea is not about to receive much support
from those who are part of the American Baptist Seminary
of the West, but it should be considered, nevertheless, as a
matter of Christian stewardship.

Colgate Rochester/Bexley Hall/Crozer Theological Seminary presently provides training for the more liberal wing of
the denomination, and that distinctive justifies its continued
existence. Besides that, it is part of a consortium of schools
that share their burdens of cost and together provide a high
quality of education for their respective students.

Andover Newton Theological School, in the Boston area,
continues to be a school very much in the moderate theological tradition, and because it is also identified with the United
Church of Christ, it has enough students and resources to
ensure its continued existence. The more conservative evangelical candidates for ministry in the New England area find

a ready home at Gordon-Conwell Theological Seminary. Like Fuller, Gordon-Conwell makes ample provisions for special courses in American Baptist church polity to meet our denominational needs for specialized training.

Even more important than the number of schools there are and what resources are available to support them is the whole question of what our seminaries offer in the way of a curriculum. For instance, there are those in the classical theological tradition who still contend that students have a need to learn Hebrew and Greek. And so it is that these courses are usually made part of a seminarian's experience. These courses are required in spite of the fact that there is general agreement that they usually prove to be little more than painful exercises in patience for those who must take them.

The idea behind promoting these disciplines is that students who learn to think in these biblical languages will have the ability to enter into the consciousness of those who wrote the Scriptures, grasping the context of Hebrew society and the settings of the early church. But seriously, how many students really learn the biblical language well enough to *think* in it?

There is a big difference between being able to translate an ancient language and being able to think in that language. Very few students can do the latter upon completion of their seminary training. The overwhelming majority end up as such poor translators that they have no choice but to rely on the work of experts. In light of all of this, would it not be better to drop Hebrew and Greek from the list of required courses? Is it not true that there are a host of books that are readily available that will help preachers to get detailed meanings of specific and crucial words of biblical texts? Is there not a general consensus that expository preaching can be sound and valid without an intensive knowledge of the original languages? The answer to all of these questions is "of course."

As a boy, the only reason I knew that my pastor had studied Greek was that he preached that familiar sermon about the three types of love: *eros, philia*, and *agape*. I doubt he used his language courses for much more than that, and truthfully, I was and am glad for that. I have an aversion to those preachers who commonly lord it over their congregations with condescending authority by intoning, "In the original Greek. . . ."

I remember Dr. Albert Williams, the longtime professor of evangelism and placement director at Eastern Baptist Theological Seminary, reading our class a letter he had received from a small church in upstate New York. "Dear Dr. Williams, " the letter began. "Our former pastor has died. We would like for you to recommend someone to take his place. Please send us the names of some candidates who do *not* know Greek and who have not been to the Holy Land."

I do not mean that a real and thorough knowledge of the biblical languages is futile. On the contrary, a preacher who can penetrate ancient culture and identify with the people who originally read and wrote the Scriptures is a rare treasure.

Indeed, I could critique other aspects of various curriculums, but my primary purpose here is not so much to criticize what our seminaries are presently teaching as it is to point out some absolutely essential things that they are *not* teaching.

They are not teaching future pastors how to build great churches. We need ministers who have the well-honed skills of entrepreneurs. When I look at the growing congregations of America, they all have pastoral leaders who grasp the basic skills of programming, marketing, and institutional organizing. There is little, if any, training provided in seminary that would teach students how to help their churches grow. Ministerial students are given the impression that if their sermons have substance to them and their Christian education programs are well developed, people will just show up.

Of course, this is not the case. A church must position itself to draw people, because, like it or not, it is competing for people's attention with all kinds of other institutions and activities, including other churches. Purists may protest that marketing is worldly and "unspiritual," but they cannot effectively argue their case from Scripture. In reality, techniques such as phone marketing and advertising via newspapers, radio, and special mailings can make a significant difference in how well the people of a community will support a given church and be a part of its ministries.

Organizational management courses are also sadly absent from the curriculum in most seminaries. There is little guidance given about how to organize and develop agendas for meetings, even though running successful meetings is a crucial ability for anyone who is going to build up a church.

Courses in conflict resolution, which experienced pastors say is an absolutely necessary skill, are also left out of the requirements for potential pastors. How many times have churches been destroyed by splits and fights simply because church elders could not figure out how to help conflicting parties work out their differences? How many good people have given up on the church or have left the pastorate because of the disillusionment that comes from power struggles within the body of Christ? The fact that our seminaries do not make training in conflict resolution an essential part of the curriculum is all the evidence needed to make the case that these schools have become "ivory tower" institutions that fail to prepare pastors for the real world.

Still another area that is sadly neglected in ministerial training is finance. Fund raising and the development of operational budgets are given only passing attention, even though virtually every church's ministry is largely dependent on its available financial resources. Pastors should be taught what goes into making a business plan. Otherwise, they will not know how to enable their congregations to carry out their respective missions. Undeniably, long-term planning is a rarity in our churches, and the scarcity of such planning is a primary reason that most mainline churches seem to be floundering.

When I was a faculty member at the Wharton School of the University of Pennsylvania, I was asked to develop a curriculum for the administration of religious institutions. Significantly, Protestant students never signed up for the courses. At that time, only Roman Catholic and Jewish leaders understood the importance of business skills for ministry. Apparently, little has changed.

Seminaries without Walls

One of the most creative innovations in the training of clergy has been the creation of seminaries without walls. Instead of candidates for the ministry going away to seminaries, most of which resemble university graduate schools, seminaries without walls train students in the context of specially selected local churches. Students are placed in learning groups of eight to twelve, each of which is based in a church setting where students can both observe and participate in a highly effective ministry.

I recently visited such a learning group organized in a large and growing church in northern California. Interestingly, four of the students came from the church itself, two of whom admitted to me that originally they had no intention of going into the ministry. They had been drawn into it through the excitement generated in their own church by the training program.

These students took only a half load of academic coursework because so much of their training was practical experience. All did church visitation, taught Sunday school, participated in committee meetings, engaged in church administration, and helped staff the youth program. In all that they did, they were observed and coached by church staff members with great expertise in these areas of ministry. The church developed a basic library for the students, but a good bit of their research reading was done at a nearby university library with which the church had established a special relationship.

This training center was also notable for its use of technology. With their personal computers, learning-group members were able to interact with students at churches in other locations. All of them participated in a special ministry training program designed by a leading seminary as well. As such technologies become more widely used, the educational possibilities of these seminaries without walls become virtually limitless.

Another benefit of seminaries without walls is that they could easily adapt to meet the needs of the commuting, often second-career, student who must live with her or his family and hold down a job while attending seminary. Obviously, many of these students could not easily relocate geographically, but with a computerized network, they could be tied into the educational process without leaving home.

One of the most attractive dimensions of a seminary without walls is that it graduates students at a fraction of the cost of a traditional seminary. The students involved will not have such huge loan debts when they graduate. Several of the students I met were going out to plant new churches. They were pleased to be free of the burdens of student loans as they moved into situations where there would be limited financial support for their work.

Again, those who have vested interests in maintaining traditional seminary education will balk at my suggestion. But I believe that the many seminaries, including those of other denominations, should be combined to set up one central learning center. This "superschool" could make available the kind of computer education programs that are the wave of the future. Faculty members could make regular visits to conduct special one-day seminars to each of the seminaries without walls connected with their denomination. Frankly, such an arrangement holds far more promise than the system we presently have in place, which often has students spend three years cogitating in an "ivory tower," only to sink or swim in a small, dying church likely to utterly destroy his or her self-confidence.

Radical Changes in Youth Ministry

Of all the failures of mainline denominations over the last three decades, none has been more pronounced than their failure in youth ministry. To say that the programs have lacked imagination would be more than kind. A generalized judgment is that youth ministry has been dead. What vitality does exist has come from programs that mainline denominational groups have borrowed from parachurch movements such as Young Life, Youth for Christ, Intervarsity Christian Fellowship, and Campus Crusade for Christ. It is not unfair to say that our seminaries haven't a clue as to how to train their students to reach teenagers and older youth. And the effects in the lives of our churches give ample evidence of this.

A revitalized youth program is crucial to the renewal of mainline denominations. The importance of reaching youth is obvious. Most major decisions as to what role Christ will play in the lives of people are made between the ages of fifteen and twenty-five. Consequently, the failure to effectively minister to this age group means that mainline denominations fail them during their most crucial years.

Our denominational churches seem out of touch with the kind of music, activities, and challenges that speak to the hearts and souls of youth. It is no wonder that we do not recruit the finest and the best of them into the pastoral ministry. Just at that time of life when they are making their vocational choices, we turn them off to the church because of our failure to address them with the gospel in any meaningful way.

One of the reasons we are failing is because we have fallen into some traps of our own making. For instance, we became overly committed to relational ministries and built our whole program with a style of teaching young people through face-to-face encounters. In our overreaction to the youth rallies of fundamentalists and the psychological manipulation of some evangelists, we rejected anything that looked like a mass meeting. We became trapped in one way of doing youth work and ridiculed all others. Mainline denominational leaders questioned, and even mocked, anything that seemed to make mass appeals to young people.

It is time for mainline denominational leaders to realize that the big events are back. Young people are flocking to Jesus festivals, Christian rock concerts, youth congresses, rallies, denominational conventions, and a host of other gatherings. The size of some of these gatherings staggers the imagination: The annual four-day Creation Festival in central Pennsylvania draws more than forty thousand young people, while the Southern Baptists of Missouri pack in over twenty thousand for an all-day celebration at a theme park outside of Kansas City.

The phenomenon is evident not only in America but also in England, where fifteen thousand young people rock and roll to music groups at Greenbelt, a Christian arts festival held just outside of London, and where more than twenty-seven thousand get together in the island's northern resort town of Prestatyn for an event called Spring Harvest. Patterned after Spring Harvest, New Zealand's Mainstage draws kids from Down Under. Even in highly secularized Australia and supposedly spiritually dead Europe, massive youth conventions are suddenly in vogue, and Christian rock festivals are often smashing successes.

Youth for Christ is rediscovering the rally. In cities across the country, young people are being drawn to gatherings reminiscent of rallies held in the forties and fifties. A special genre of youth speakers, now called "great communicators," belt out an old-time religion spiced with Cosby-like humor and a hip vocabulary. After a hiatus of evangelistic methods nurtured by relational theology, we are finding that young people we thought were beyond such appeals are going down the aisles to the strains of "Just as I Am." Even Campus Crusade for Christ has gotten into the big-event act. This organization still makes a one-on-one presentation of the Four Spiritual Laws its mainstay, but it also sponsors huge youth congresses and conventions.

Mainstream denominations are just now rediscovering young people's current fascination with a style of evangelism that seemed all but written off by the late fifties. Recently, in the Atlanta Superdome, I spoke to a gathering of more than thirty-five thousand young people from congregations of the Evangelical Lutheran Church of America. It was the kind of mass rally that would have thrilled the heart of Billy Graham.

Religious Woodstock

It's an oversimplification to define these gatherings as Christian replications of the rock festivals and concerts promoted by the secular community, despite obvious parallels that invite such an easy explanation. Certainly the Jesus festivals (as they have come to be called) look like religious Woodstocks. Creation, Jesus Northwest, Fishnet, and the like, are set up, in most instances, outside urban centers—at farms, pastures, and rural parks—and feature religious rock bands on the main stage. Reminiscent of the countercultural gatherings of the spaced-out, dropped-out generation that replaced the social protesters of the sixties, modern religious attenders camp out, dress in raggedy clothes, and look a whole lot like their predecessors. Religious rock vibrates at every meeting of these festivals, and the crowds scream and gyrate to drums and guitars.

The popularity of the groups that play and sing the new sound of contemporary Christian music has no doubt contributed to the development of many of these festivals. Christian radio stations have elevated groups like Petra and The Rez Band to celebrity status. The multimillion-dollar Christian record business has made collector's items of releases by Amy Grant and Michael W. Smith. Add to this the promotional paraphernalia of T-shirts and buttons and whatnot, and we have on our hands hot rock stars who are able to generate enthusiasm in young people for the things of God.

However (before we are tempted to easy comparisons and simplistic parallels), I should note that in some instances these gatherings resemble nineteenth-century camp meetings more than rock festivals. Spring Harvest, the ever-growing English extravaganza, is focused wholly on preaching and teaching and has no special-music groups. Awesome congregational singing rather than soloists lift up hymns to God. Spring Harvest even holds its meetings under a gigantic tent—complete with a sawdust trail. Other big events have similar elements of what many thought was an outdated style of evangelism. Obviously, a more sophisticated analysis of these and other big events is needed to explain their sudden popularity.

Collective Effervescence

Social realists (or social holists, as they are sometimes called in the field of sociology) might be able to lend some interesting insights to the subject of mass meetings. Leaders of this perspective of social reality, from the great modern sociologist Emile Durkheim to the present, have always been convinced that at large gatherings, something happens—something that transcends what the people at these events could ever experience as individuals. Durkheim explained that large gatherings of people stimulated to interact in a spirited fashion are capable of producing what he called a "collective effervescence." This collective effervescence, in turn, is likely to compel participants to behave in ways foreign to their individual personalities.

Before we contend that Durkheim and his successors are describing mere mob psychosis, let me strongly suggest that this phenomenon is much more subtle than we may realize. While social holists don't claim to be mystics, they are nevertheless aware that when individuals interact in some group settings, they collectively manifest traits that transcend the traits inherent in those who make up the group. These collective traits can't be traced to or reduced to the traits of the individuals. Collective traits seem to have a life of their own (Durkheim considered them "things in themselves"), and all the participants integrated with the group are affected by them.

This discovery can be good news to youth workers. According to social holists, certain positive religious traits and beliefs—traits that people greatly need but may be unable to generate on their own—can emerge *sui generis* (of its own kind) in large groups. Faith, for instance, may be hard for some individuals to muster by themselves, but when they are in a group that expresses faith as part of its collective effervescence, they may find themselves full of faith.

Nearly a century ago the American psychologist William James wrote in his classic *Varieties of Religious Experience* that the makeup of some personalities renders them much less capable than others of believing in an invisible God. Faith and other fruits of the Spirit (joy and love come immediately to mind) may be more easily cultivated by collective effervescence than in isolation. In short, a large group can enable certain people to be and do what they might otherwise find impossible. Youth workers who have failed to elicit faith from some teenagers may find that faith comes easily at a Billy Graham evangelistic crusade. A bitter young person who experiences neither joy nor love might experience both in the context of a charismatic Jesus festival.

I am not attempting to reduce the work of the Holy Spirit to a sociological process. I am simply pointing out that God

can and does use the collective effervescence of large gatherings of Christians to communicate to particular people. One
need look no further than Promise Keepers to recognize the
power of this phenomenon to impact even married, middle-
aged men, a group supposedly immune to such open, religious
fervor. Such events are often even more decisive for young
people in search of identity and belonging.

Obviously, mainline denominations need to more actively
and effectively promote their own large youth gatherings,
incorporating the best parts of the most successful existing
events. These events not only have the potential to transform
kids into committed Christians, but also to create a strong,
collective enthusiasm and loyalty for the churches and denominations that sponsor them.

Evangelistic Styles for Youth

Evangelization of youth is crucial, but there is a great
disagreement about how it should be done. Some emphasize
being "saved" and entering into a personal relationship with
Jesus. Others downplay efforts to solicit converts and focus
outreach on working for social justice—which, they feel, gives
evidence that the kingdom of God is manifesting itself in
history. Some Christians try to reach out to the world through
tracts, radio broadcasts, and street meetings, while others
witness by example.

Debate over style and objectives of outreach can be intense,
at times resulting in name calling and schisms. Many Christian groups have developed theologies to legitimate various
styles of outreach, and to them, these theologies become as
sacred as the gospel message itself.

The Influence of Socioeconomic Status
on Evangelistic Style

What many mainline denominations fail to recognize is
that socioeconomic factors often influence styles of evangelism more than either the Bible or the Holy Spirit. In his book

The Social Sources of Denominationalism, H. Richard Niebuhr, a prominent sociologist and theologian of a generation ago, identified a variety of these factors and demonstrated how they condition the forms and styles of outreach and evangelism throughout Christendom. Niebuhr showed that of all the sociological influences on outreach styles, none had a more significant influence than the socioeconomic status of group members. He found that the class identity of a given group determined, more than anything else, how that group would relate to the society in which it was set.

Using a typology borrowed from the German sociologist Ernst Troeltsch, Niebuhr suggested that the religious style of the lower socioeconomic classes could be identified as *sectarian*, while the religious style of the middle to upper classes could be labeled *ecclesiastic*. (In America, ecclesiastic religion is usually associated with mainline denominationalism.) According to Niebuhr, these two religious types are found at opposite ends of a continuum. Each has a specific, socially prescribed world view that expresses itself in a specific and distinctive style of evangelism.

The distinctive world views of sectarian and ecclesiastic Christians, drawn from their respective socioeconomic environments, radically affect how each group views the society they are attempting to influence for Christ. Those world views particularly affect how each group believes the converts should live out their faith in the world.

Sectarian Evangelism: Brother, Are You Saved?

Members of sectarian groups are generally drawn from what Niebuhr called the "socially disinherited" parts of the population. Sectarians tend to come from the less prestigious areas of their respective communities. They often dominate the lower-paying jobs and are, for the most part, less educated than those who align with more ecclesiastical religious groups such as the mainline denominations of Protestant Christianity.

Growing up with a sense of social disinheritance can generate a counteraction against society. Sectarians tend to put down the society they feel has rejected them. Sectarian youth groups often express their rejection of the world by establishing a pietistic lifestyle they label "holy." They contrast their lifestyle with what they consider to be the "worldly" lifestyle typical of middle-class America.

This pietistic sectarian lifestyle is easy to identify. It manifests itself in a rejection of rock music, smoking, drinking, dancing, and other behavior considered evil—even demonically inspired—and designed to stimulate the "lusts of the flesh." The language of the sectarian youth group differs from that of the world; a special religious vocabulary comes into play—romantic dates are "times of fellowship" and decisions are "leadings of the Lord."

The evangelistic task of sectarian youth leaders is never complete until their young people are socialized into this mind-set. They must direct their converts away from what they consider to be humanistic thought and behavior and toward "the truth." The leader's efforts are most successful when they culminate in their youth-group members going on to higher education at Bible schools or colleges that espouse their separatist lifestyle.

The style of evangelistic outreach generated by this world view encourages individual decisions that result in personal conversion to the Christian faith. Sectarians will use any ethical means available to promote the truths they see as the core of the gospel message. Sectarian outreach often includes, for example, tract distribution and neon signs that declare to a lost world that "Jesus saves." Sectarians believe that faith comes from hearing the message, and the message is heard through the word of God (Romans 10:17).

Sectarians have an urgency about their outreach efforts, built on the assumption that their way of salvation is the only way. Sectarians are haunted by their belief that every day thousands of people die and go to hell because they didn't believe in Jesus. The love and concern sectarians feel for the lost drives them to use all methods available to save people from a Christless eternity. They admit that grabbing sinners by their coat labels and asking, "Buddy, are you saved?" might be a bit aggressive, but they claim that at least it shows they care.

As mainline denominations reach out and incorporate churches from the inner city into their memberships, they will find that these churches bring with them sectarian styles of youth evangelism. Those in charge of youth ministry simply must not look down on this kind of evangelistic outreach. Mainline denominations can no longer afford elitist arrogance. They must remove from positions of leadership those people who disdain this other kind of evangelism.

Ecclesiastic Evangelism:
Let's Change the World Together

In mainline churches, those who design youth ministry programs are usually in what sociologists would call the ecclesiastic mold. Ecclesiastic youth leaders project a more accommodating attitude toward the dominant culture than their sectarian counterparts. They are eager to prove that they can be "cool" in the eyes of typical teenagers. They promote the idea that a Christian lifestyle can be culturally normal.

Ecclesiastic youth groups seek to socialize their members into the dominant values of the culture. They operate on the assumption that American society was designed to be just; people experience discrimination and oppression when the social system doesn't function as it was designed to do.

Those who develop the ideologies and programs for these youth groups contend that central to Christian youth ministry is the challenge to improve the social order so that the ideals of America (which are often viewed as being synonymous with the principles of justice cited in the Scriptures) might be realized. Peter Berger, one of the leaders in the field of sociology of religion, contends that ecclesiastic Christians view the world as okay and define the task of the church as improving a basically good world so that the inadequacies that do exist in the American social system can be overcome.

For the ecclesiastic-type youth program, which has become typical in most mainline denominations, there is a strong emphasis on getting teenagers involved in social action programs. Short-term mission trips in which young people can get their hands dirty repairing a church or school building in a Third World country are ideal activities to sponsor. Middle-class teenagers readily participate in efforts that they believe can make a difference in the world. Furthermore, they regularly report that in ministries that enable them to help the poor, they themselves are changed. These involvements in social ministries often are faith-generating experiences. Many youth workers from mainline denominational churches report that such short-term mission trips do more for their young people than all the other programs combined that they run throughout the year.

Taking the Best from Both

What lessons can we learn from our observation of the two religious styles that dominate our culture? More important, how shall we approach outreach in our ministries? God uses both sectarian and ecclesiastic Christians to accomplish His purposes, regardless of the weaknesses inherent in each style. Yet we may vastly strengthen both the effectiveness and maturity of our own outreach efforts when we synthesize what is strong from both traditions and establish a more holistic approach to evangelism. No matter what background we come from, we can see that there is much to respect and imitate in that "other" tradition that may seem so foreign to us.

For example, many—if not most—ecclesiastic Christians who put down the aggressive evangelistic style of sectarian religion admit that they themselves became dedicated Christians through affiliating with the very kind of sectarian program they now condemn. While speaking at a mainline denominational seminary recently, I asked my audience how many of them had become Christians through sectarian-type evangelistic programs. More than two-thirds of those present raised their hands. Though some of us may be uncomfortable with what we see as "simplistic" evangelism, without it, many of us wouldn't be where we are today.

On the other hand, sectarians must recognize that "getting saved" is more than getting set up for the next life. Salvation should be viewed as enlistment in a movement committed to transforming this world into the kind of world God wills for it to be. God loves this world and wants to make it into His kingdom. God wants all "principalities and powers" transformed into social structures that will serve God's purposes and be a blessing to all humanity. Conversion should be seen as a process through which young people can become God's agents of change in this world.

For this to happen, young people must be converted to Christ *and* become his agents for a nonviolent revolution that will challenge the present order of things and struggle for the realization of God's kingdom within history. This kind of outreach requires zealous, Spirit-filled converts committed to a vision of the world inspired by the biblical revelation. When our outreach programs generate such converts, the dichotomy between personalistic salvation and social transformation will disappear. We will see a powerful linking of the evangelistic imperatives of sectarian Christians and the social concerns of ecclesiastic believers—the holistic outreach strategy that has been God's wonderful plan from the beginning.

All of this may seem like just a lot of talk about sociology and theology. The practical question might be raised as to just what it is that mainline denominations are supposed to do in the face of these seemingly abstract challenges that I have outlined. What kinds of Christian education materials must be created to help teach children and young people to balance the individual and social aspects of their faith? How can we train youth workers to understand and reach the very different youth subcultures of our day? With the resources of

mainline denominations dwindling along with their memberships, how can we afford to retool our youth ministries to
reverse this tide?

First of all, it is clear to me that mainline denominations
should stop even trying to produce their own Sunday school
curriculums and youth ministry training events. That work
is already being done for them by large, specialized parachurch organizations and Christian publishing houses. Every
year, companies like Zondervan, Urban Ministries, Inc., and
David C. Cook put out a wide variety of youth and children's
Sunday school materials catering to the needs of a broad
range of congregations. This material is generally excellent
in both biblical content and ease of use. It could be argued
that such curriculums do not address the specific distinctives
of particular denominations, but even this difficulty can be
overcome through cooperation and creativity. For instance,
my own denomination, American Baptist Churches, U.S.A.,
has entered into an excellent cooperative relationship with
the David C. Cook company. Instead of expending its own
resources producing all of its own materials, the ABC offers
to its churches curriculum produced by David C. Cook. In
turn, David C. Cook personnel regularly meet with ABC's
executives in charge of the development of church schools to
make sure that our denomination's particular theological
and social concerns will be addressed and included in the
material that is recommended to our churches. Using their
collective purchasing power, other denominations can establish
similar relationships with publishers, eliminating the many
costs of producing their own Christian education materials.

There may still be a need for denominations to provide
curriculum supplements, formed on specific theology, polity,
and church heritage. But the days when mainline denominations ruled the roost and could afford to expend vast amounts
of energy and resources creating complete catalogs of in-
house Christian education materials have long passed away.

The same is true of youth ministry training. Parachurch
organizations and companies like Youth Specialties, Group

Publishing, SouLife, and The National Institute of Youth Ministry offer an incredible array of learning opportunities for both professional and lay youth workers.

Youth Specialties' National Youth Workers Conventions are widely recognized as sponsoring brilliantly organized events that bring together the very best youth-ministry practitioners, speakers, consultants, programs, and resources. On the inner-city front, Kingdomworks' Urban Youth Workers Convention does the same thing. There are other national gatherings, as well, along with regional training seminars, and local networks, all supported by an overwhelming array of music, videos, books, and other publications designed to equip Christian youth workers to reach this new generation of kids. *Group* magazine alone has a curriculum of more than two hundred books on youth ministry.

Significantly, most of the youth workers taking advantage of these resources and attending these gatherings are already from mainline denominations. What is needed is for mainline denominations to more directly cooperate and promote these parachurch programs. Those who participate in these truly ecumenical events consistently say they learn more about reaching kids in them than they do at any denominational function or in their seminary training.

For many years, church leaders were deeply suspicious of parachurch organizations, often justifiably convinced that the people who ran them were embittered and biased against mainline denominations. More recently, however, such suspicions have been diminished as parachurch organizations have demonstrated an increasingly respectful and cooperative attitude toward mainline churches. Increasingly, parachurch youth ministries, recognizing their own inherent limitations, see themselves as support systems for local churches. Likewise, denominational leaders are waking up to find that these parachurch ministries represent some of their best and brightest hopes for developing strong and effective youth ministries into the twenty-first century.

Prescription 4

Restructuring Local Churches for the Twenty-first Century

We now must face the fact that the average, ordinary local church that has typified mainline denominations throughout the twentieth century is increasingly unable to meet the desires of the people we need to reach in the twenty-first century. The so-called superchurches have made the average local church outdated and noncompetitive in America's religious marketplace.

Unlike the typical mainline churches, which are considered more than healthy if they have three to four hundred in attendance at every Sunday morning worship service, superchurches have congregations that can number in the thousands. I have preached in one superchurch that registers more than fifteen thousand at their weekly worship services (they have three services to accommodate the crowds). Already in America, according to John Vaughan of the International Megachurch Research Center of Southwest Baptist University, there are 270 churches with average weekly congregations of more than two thousand. And a new church joins this groups every two to three weeks. These churches are the wave of the future because they are equipped to meet the variety of needs that are everywhere evident in our stressed-out society.

Because superchurches are so large, they have the resources to provide the host of special services and programs that people believe they must have in order to "make it" in their everyday lives. In one superchurch I visited in southern California, there are courses in parenting, a special ministry to divorced persons, a support group for parents of homosexuals, programs on how to handle codependence, and other specialized study groups too numerous to list. The place is a religious supermarket. All of these programs are of high quality. Each has a specially trained leader. These programs are in addition to what this church considers its regular program, which offers the following:

1. *A Singles Program.* This includes a weekly meeting that brings together between three hundred and five hundred business and professional singles to hear an outstanding speaker and to socialize. There are special Sunday school classes geared to the needs of single persons, and a variety of social outings. There are weekend spiritual-renewal retreats and ski retreats. There are outreach programs that offer singles the opportunities to visit shut-ins, build low-cost housing for the poor, go on short-term mission trips to Third World countries, and engage in a host of other challenging ways to serve the less fortunate. Two full-time ministers are provided to supervise these activities and to offer special counseling to singles who are having personal problems. This ministry is designed for singles from twenty-five to thirty-five years of age, and participants can meet Christians who are potential marriage partners.

2. *A College and Career Program.* In many ways this program is like the one offered to singles, but the emphasis here is on college-age youth. The music and speakers for the weekly meetings are all geared to be relevant to young people in this age bracket. Full-time ministers who have special expertise in working with college-age youth give leadership to this program, and the church provides an operating budget that is well over $100,000 per year.

3. *High School and Junior High School Programs.* Allow-

ing no cost to stand in its way, this superchurch has hired the experts in ministry to teenagers. They know that parents are desperate to find churches that will do something for these young people. Christian rock musicians are frequently brought in for special concerts. Films produced especially for teenagers are regularly shown. The array of rallies, conferences, retreats, and conventions that these young people are taken to regularly is far too wide to list.

4. *Sports Programs.* This church has its own gym and a full-time sports director who makes sure that there are leagues for almost every sport and for just about every age group. There are a variety of sports banquets for handing out trophies for winners and regular "chapels" in which Christian principles are applied to athletics.

5. *Music Programs.* This church has five full-time musicians on its staff. There are youth choirs, children's choirs, bell choirs, an orchestra, and gospel quartets to go along with its regular chancel choir. The music produced is polished with professional skill. The choir is so good that during the Christmas season they put on a special program called "The Singing Christmas Tree." More than a dozen performances of this program play to sold-out crowds that number more than ten thousand at each performance.

6. *Home Bible Studies.* Every member of the church is urged to be part of a home Bible study group that usually meets weekly. Thousands of church members attend these meetings conducted by professional ministers who have made small-group ministry the focus of their energies. Members often find that these small groups become caring communities that love them and look after them in special ways. It is fair to say that the personal attention and pastoral care that is received in these small, home Bible studies (usually numbering between fifteen and twenty participants) rivals what can be found under the auspices of the smaller churches that claim to make such concerns their forte.

7. *Counseling Services.* This particular church has three full-time counselors on its staff. Trained in the skills of

psychotherapy, and having integrated their counseling techniques with biblical principles, these counselors are able to provide expert help to people with marriage problems, troubled teenagers, those who face career crises, and many others.

Ordinary Churches Are Out of the Running

Already, many pastors of ordinary traditional churches feel threatened by these superchurches. One of my former students who interviewed for the pastorate of a Baptist church of 350 members, located in the suburbs of Chicago, told me, "You won't believe what the pulpit committee was expecting of me. They wanted me to guarantee them that I could be a polished preacher, an effective youth leader, an expert family counselor, a good fund raiser, and a clever business manager, as well as being able to provide leadership in an extensive program of visitation evangelism." This pulpit committee was expecting one man to enable their church to compete with all the services and programs being offered by a whole team of ministers and other professionals at the superchurch in the same community.

Superchurches simply outclass ordinary churches. Vaughan suggests that they are a whole new development in Christianity that will change forever what Americans expect that churches will do for them. I am convinced that traditional mainline churches will decline in size and importance in the face of this competition.

Among the various staff members of a superchurch in my Philadelphia suburb there is one full-time minister who does nothing but minister to the children of broken marriages. A divorcée I know who was going to the local Methodist church transferred her membership to this superchurch. She told me, "I had to do it. Raising two boys alone is more than I can handle. Ralph [the special pastor for children of divorced parents] gives me some help, and I need all the help I can get."

In the face of the challenges that are presented by the superchurches, those of us in mainline denominations need

not despair. First of all, there is ample reason to believe that
with the proper leadership, we could create some superchurches of our own. Denominational labels neither bring
people into those congregations nor keep them out. The
programs and the pastoral leadership are what count, and
there are many cases when we can match the ministries of
the nondenominational superchurches in each and every
respect.

Granted, some of these mainline churches find it desirable
to drop their denominational name, even while holding on
to their denominational affiliation. There are Baptist churches
that now call themselves "Christian Life Centers" and Presbyterian churches that call themselves "Community Churches,"
but they are mainline churches, nevertheless.

Second, there will always be some people who prefer small-
and medium-sized congregations simply because of the greater
opportunity for participation they provide. Becoming an
important part of the ministry of a medium-sized mainline denominational church brings special rewards. The personal satisfaction of being a genuine pillar of the church, for
instance, would be difficult to experience in a mega-sized
congregation.

The third possibility, which I believe is the best hope for
mainline denominational growth and development, is to create a vast network of house churches. This back-to-the-future
approach to church planting, rooted in the New Testament,
is ideally suited to thrive in the kind of society currently
taking shape in America. In the midst of a massive, overpowering, impersonal social order, house churches offer alienated
people precisely the kind of intimate religious and social
experience they are looking for.

There is no single best model for planting such house
churches. The settings in which they are established will
determine which practices are most effective for attracting
members and meeting their needs. Also, the gifts and abilities
of the individuals involved must play a major role in determining the kind of ministries that should be established.

There are some who are brilliant practitioners of contemporary worship. Others who have expertise in community organization can bring people together to address the social concerns of their communities. There are still others whose gifts enable them to create a sense of caring *koinonia* among people hungry for fellowship. One thing is certain, however; Bible study must be a dominant feature of these new house churches. Simply stated, millions of people are hungry for Bible knowledge. They are biblically illiterate, and they want to do something about it. Especially among baby boomers there is a very strong desire to find out what the Scriptures say and how they apply to everyday life.

This Bible study, however, cannot be constricted by fundamentalists intent on prooftexting some ultraconservative, highly legalistic lifestyle. That will not work at all. Such rigid, nostalgic prescriptions are irrelevant to baby boomers and even more so to Generation X-ers struggling to face the complicated challenges of their stressed-out lives. While they respect the authority of the Bible as God's Word to them, they cannot and do not approach it like a straightforward book of rules and regulations.

A sociological survey will reveal that most people are what can best be described as "functionalist inerrantists." Confronted with the question, Do you think that everything in the Bible is literally true? most of these people would answer with some hesitation, "Well, not really." Nevertheless, they are more than ready to acknowledge that the Bible is a special message from God and is *the* place to turn for truth, solutions to their problems, and the way of salvation. When they read the Bible, they accept its words as inspired by God. They may admit they have problems believing that the Bible is literally true word for word, but they still treat it that way as they read and study it. When Billy Graham thunders from the pulpit, "The Bible says...," they accept what follows as having the authority of divine revelation. Precisely because they regard the Bible so highly, they want first and foremost to know what it says and how it applies to their lives.

Therefore, a denominational house church movement, combining the intimacy and personal care of small groups with the attraction of genuine Bible study, could very well become even more popular than superchurches in the days to come. But we must mobilize our people to make it happen.

To make our own denomination effective in doing what needs to be done in this special ministry of house church planting, we have to find a lot of highly committed laypersons. We need at least one thousand married couples or teams of singles willing to leave whatever they are doing and completely commit themselves to this unique kind of church planting. That may sound unrealistic, but I know there are plenty of people out there who are ready to serve. We simply have not challenged them! For example, one-third of American men between fifty-five and sixty-four years of age have already taken early retirement. We must take advantage of this huge pool of potential Christian workers by inspiring and training them for ministry. Wherever new communities are built, we must have teams of workers ready to immediately move in to establish local churches. These church-planting units could be supplied with summer volunteer teams ready to run outreach programs for children and go door to door inviting people into small-group fellowships.

The first house church meeting would be called only when ten people from the community were ready to join the church-planting couple in a weekly Bible study. It was no accident that Jesus put together a group of twelve followers to be the basic unit for planting his church in Jerusalem. Experts in small-group dynamics can give a host of reasons why a group of twelve is ideal for positive interaction.

Until there are ten recruits, the church-planting couples would do well to make regular house calls to maintain the support of those who show interest. These calls ought not to be filled with small talk, but rather should be times of meaningful discussion about the Bible, real-life problems, and what people hope the coming church will do for them.

The leaders of these house churches must know what they

are doing. They have to understand small-group dynamics and not make these get-togethers into miniature versions of traditional worship services. They must avoid the temptation to lecture the other members. They must be able to share the truth of the gospel in a way that allows all members to share their own insights, reflections, and questions. They must learn to control without manipulating or seizing control.

What follows should be growth by fission. As groups get going, every effort should be made to have the members bring along new friends and acquaintances. When the group reaches twenty members, it is then time to split it and begin the process again.

The church-planting couple ought not to try to lead more than four groups. Indeed, the nurture of four groups will likely push them to the limits of their time and energy. Before they try to do any more, they should call for help or, better still, mentor into leadership roles some of those involved in their ministry.

It is easy to see where this plan leads. With new cell units regularly being created, a given community will soon become full of them. Eventually, some members of those groups will propose that these various house churches contribute money for building a sanctuary. The idea of unifying the groups and worshiping together as one big fellowship will become tremendously attractive. Nevertheless, the proposal ought to be resisted. Building a sanctuary is a bad idea! First of all, it costs too much money. The dollars eaten up in constructing a building could be better used adding staff members. In our contemporary society, people expect to have a variety of specialized social, personal, and spiritual needs met by the ministers of the church. For instance, the availability of a highly trained expert in youth work could make a house church extremely attractive to parents of teenagers. Also, having someone on the staff with expertise in counseling would enable these house churches to meet some essential personal needs for people in the community.

Specialists could be hired to offer ministries to singles and senior citizens. Having someone to run a day-care service would help these house churches solve a crucial community problem: what to do to help single parents who have nine-to-five jobs. What would have been spent on a building could support staff workers in these ministries. It will be these specialized ministries, not necessarily a new building, that will increase the effectiveness of this house church ministry program.

Second, it would be better to redirect the energies of those who want to build a building into mission projects. Money used for missions provides more gratification for the givers than they are likely to get from having their money used to put up a sanctuary.

Christians are growing increasingly cynical about investing in bricks and mortar. They want to invest in people. They want to see lives touched with ministries of love. They want to see the hungry fed, the naked clothed, and those in prisons loved back into lives filled with hope.

Sometimes when I am preaching, I ask this rhetorical question: If Jesus had the choice between spending a million dollars on putting up a new building or using that money to feed hungry children in Haiti, which do you think he would choose to do? Always the response leaves no doubt that people believe his priority would be to feed the Haitian kids.

Constructing church buildings is sometimes necessary, but in most situations, building is a risk that often leads to a gigantic waste of money. Communities change too fast these days. If a building is constructed to house the kind of programs that a given church has today, it is likely to be obsolete within a few decades.

Moreover, the ethnic, socioeconomic, and religious identities of communities can change so rapidly that the church demographics may vary greatly from year to year. Consequently, a building that was designed for a congregation of several hundred could soon end up an empty barn in which a few dozen people rattle around. I watched this happen to the church in which I was reared.

The New Berean Baptist Church had a sanctuary that could seat four hundred people easily. But our neighborhood changed. We ended up with only sixty-five regularly attending members. Eventually we disbanded the congregation and sold the building because the families that were left did not have the financial means to maintain the building and pay the pastor's salary. We probably could have kept the church going if we had sold the building and restructured ourselves into house churches, but the idea never occurred to us.

Do not jump to the conclusion that I believe corporate worship has no place in the church of the future. On the contrary, I believe the various house churches in a community need to gather regularly for corporate worship experiences. Everything that we have learned about church growth suggests that corporate worship is absolutely essential. In some cases we should follow models laid down by the charismatic renewal movement, replacing the organ with a live band and providing a good mixture of traditional hymns with contemporary worship music.

Bringing together house churches for corporate worship does not necessarily have to happen every week, but even if it did, there would be no need to build special buildings just to house these periodic get-togethers. The best idea is to rent existing facilities. A high school gym or an auditorium will do just fine. The ballroom or the banquet hall of a local hotel can also meet the need. To pay a few hundred dollars each time you schedule worship is very different from paying the huge expenditures that go with building and maintaining a traditional sanctuary.

Other programs that require rented facilities might be jointly sponsored by these house churches. Athletic and music programs and church dinners can all be so accommodated.

One congregation I know wanted to put on a daily vacation Bible school program, so they simply rented a huge tent and put it up on a conveniently located vacant lot for a couple of weeks. The kids in the neighborhood loved it.

The image of that tent reminds me of the children of Israel wandering in the wilderness and setting up their tent tabernacle wherever they happened to be, which is a great metaphor for what the contemporary church should be. People in today's world are constantly on the move. Approximately 20 percent of all Americans move in any given year. That is roughly forty million people. The church must be mobile enough to move with them and flexible enough to constantly develop relevant, new programs to meet their needs. Big buildings are no longer the way to provide anything but big bills.

To conservative church leaders who are committed to traditional ways of doing things, such ideas may seem outlandish and impractical, but versions of them already are working across the United States. The time has come to make daring experiments. The future of mainline denominations and, more importantly, the future of Christianity in America depends on it.

Realigning the Churches

The time has come to publicly declare what most of us privately acknowledged long ago: denominational labels are virtually meaningless.

When I tell someone I am an American Baptist, I have told them next to nothing about what sort of Christian I am or what sort of church I attend. My denominational label does not say whether my church is liberal, conservative, or fundamentalist in its approach to the Bible. Identifying myself as a Baptist gives no hint whether I embrace liberation theology or the reconstruction movement, nor does it make clear my positions on abortion, homosexual marriages, or issues of personal piety. It doesn't even say just how my church goes about worshiping God on Sunday mornings.

Mainline denominations need to be groupings of churches with shared traditions, theological convictions, social values, worship styles, and overall missions. Now, within any given denomination there are many churches so vastly different from one another that one might fairly wonder if they are truly part of the same religion.

Such diversity is often celebrated in the rhetoric of denominational leaders, who claim their denominations draw strength from the unique contributions of their very different individuals and congregations. But in reality, those same leaders spend much of their energy struggling to hold their divergent churches together in the face of deep diversity, verbal warfare, and often vicious denominational politics. As one denominational leader sarcastically told me, "When we sang 'Onward Christian Soldiers' at our last convention, the people really meant it." And an American Baptist leader humorously commented, "Whenever somebody tells me he would never be a part of organized religion, I tell him that he ought to become a Baptist."

For local churches, the consequence of this diversity is sometimes disastrous. I have heard many pastors claim that their churches are not growing because denominational leaders fail to provide the kind of cohesive leadership that they need. Diminishing attendance and memberships in their churches is blamed on the chaos that prevails at the top of the denomination. While what goes on at the denominational level generally is not one of the primary factors in determining the level of effectiveness of the ministry in a given local church, it often becomes a tremendous distraction and a real obstacle to growth.

Sometimes pastors are so frustrated by the various theologies and practices in their denomination that they band together to do something about it. In the case of the Southern Baptist Convention, the conservative wing of the denomination decided that the much-lauded diversity within their ranks was not a good thing, and they organized a takeover of their denomination. As described earlier in this book, these conservatives have gained control of the decision-making process and have begun purging from the leadership of both their denomination and the teaching staffs of their seminaries those who do not agree with what they believe are the true, orthodox beliefs and practices. The moderates in the SBC have suddenly found themselves *personae non gratae* within their own denomination and in reaction have established what are essentially denominations within a denomination—the Alliance of Baptists and the Cooperative Baptist Fellowship. Of the two, the Cooperative Baptist Fellowship, at this point, seems to be stronger. This fellowship will probably become the primary organization that brings together those Southern Baptists who, because of the conservative takeover, have lost their spiritual home.

The Cooperative Baptist Fellowship represents a significant constituency of almost fifteen hundred contributing churches and over twenty-three hundred contributing individuals. These dissident Baptists can by no means be characterized as theological modernists or liberals, although most fundamentalists would call them just that. They simply do not believe there ought to be any kind of doctrinal litmus test to determine who should or should not be regarded as legitimate members of their denomination. They believe that the imposition of credal statements and standards on Southern Baptist institutions is contrary to basic baptistic principles going all the way back to Roger Williams, the founder of the Baptist movement in America.

Interestingly, the situation is reversed among American Baptist Churches, where what Southern Baptists call "moderates" predominate and conservatives feel frustrated and left out. Denominational leaders of the ABC have made tremendous efforts to keep both sides together, but the alliances they have established are tenuous, at best.

It seems to me that the best solution is for these two great Baptist denominations to consider a dramatic realignment of their churches. On the one hand, there are conservative American Baptist churches that probably would be much happier as part of the Southern Baptist Convention. On the other hand, there is little doubt that those churches that make up the Cooperative Baptist Fellowship of the SBC would be much more at home in the ABC.

Amazingly enough, such realignment could actually take place without any great upset or distraction to local pastors and their congregations, through a wonderful Baptist concept called *dual alignment*.

There are no legal barriers to any Baptist church being a member of both the Southern Baptist Convention and the American Baptist Churches simultaneously. Some churches are already so aligned. The extent to which such a church cooperates with either denomination in programming and giving is totally the prerogative of its membership. In other words, a moderate congregation in the SBC can simultaneously hold membership in the ABC and decide for itself which programs of either denomination it wants to support. How much money it chooses to give either denomination is likewise a decision belonging solely to the local church.

It is interesting to note that there is a precedent for such an arrangement. Most of the churches that make up the District of Columbia Baptist Convention have had an ongoing dual alignment with both the ABC and the SBC for more than a century, but that does not mean that these churches have had split loyalties. While maintaining such dual denominational memberships, they have, for the most part, tended to function as though they were exclusively Southern Baptist. They have generally used SBC Sunday school materials and have given their missionary funds to Southern Baptist causes. There is no reason those churches in the ABC that would rather be in the SBC could not follow the example of the D.C. Convention and establish a similar dual alignment.

Conversely and more significantly, the moderate churches of the SBC could become dually aligned with the ABC. Over time these moderate churches would be able to shift their allegiance and support the ABC. Beyond that, the entire Cooperative Baptist Fellowship and the Alliance of Baptists could enter into the membership of the ABC.

Such a realignment would certainly make everybody happier. The levels of tension that presently exist within these two denominations would diminish, and the possibility of unity for each would be greatly enhanced.

Some may ask, "Why bother with all of this dual alignment stuff? Why not just have those churches that are dissatisfied with what is going on in their respective denominations withdraw completely and join up with the other group that is more closely reflective of their beliefs and agenda for ministry?"

There are two answers. First is the matter of retirement benefits for ministers. A Southern Baptist pastor who has had yearly contributions made by his or her church through the Annuity Board would lose some of the retirement benefits that would be due at retirement if his or her church withdrew from the SBC. Through dual alignment, this problem would be overcome. Dual alignment would give the same kind of positive benefits for the pastor of an American Baptist congregation that preferred to be in the Southern Baptist Convention. (Unfortunately, this may all be a superfluous discussion in light of some recent discussions among SBC leaders. Presently a resolution is being considered that would force some pastors in the SBC being covered by the Annuity Board to find other means of providing for retirement. To put it more bluntly, the moderates may be thrown out of the group that benefits from the SBC retirement plan.)

Second, there are those in the pews who might be dissatisfied with their denomination but who, for emotional and sentimental reasons would be opposed to completely withdrawing from denominational membership. Some would say, "My parents belonged to this denomination and so did my grandparents, and I'm going to be a member until the day I die!"

Traditions are important and ought to be respected. Dual alignment is a compromise that could provide some solace to those who hold religious traditions dear and want to maintain the title of them, no matter what.

While realignment may have varied appeal for particular churches, it may be the only hope for the ABC itself. Frankly, the ABC is in serious financial trouble. Membership in the white middle-class churches that have traditionally made up its main base of support has been dropping off. Right now, the future of the ABC looks very bleak. At its national offices in Valley Forge, the pain caused by necessary budget cutbacks is inescapable. An influx of members and support from moderate SBC churches joining the ABC could give this troubled denomination just the shot in the arm it needs to make a dramatic turnaround. The new vitality gained from this arrangement could shake the ABC out of its lethargy and restore it to dynamic life.

At the same time, the benefit to the moderate Southern Baptists joining the ABC would be enormous. Rather than expending huge amounts of time and energy creating all the substructures of a new denomination, they could take advantage of the ABC's already existing national headquarters, leadership hierarchies, publishing arrangements, and tremendously effective missions program. The excitement of such a great coming together would also be a tremendous encouragement to moderates hurt by their rejection by conservative Southern Baptists. It is hard for any moderate movement to generate the kind of intense commitment, urgency, and revolutionary fervor characteristic of extremists. My sense is that both the Cooperative Baptist Fellowship and the Alliance of Baptists are suffering from a lack of purpose and dynamic energy. Joining with the ABC in order to create a new, great alliance of nonfundamentalist Baptists might cure that in a hurry.

Bureaucracies tend to be anything but bold and imaginative, even when their own survival is at stake. A radical realignment like this one I have described will not happen unless and until some truly charismatic leaders rise up in the ABC and among moderate Southern Baptists to lead the charge.

Over the past ten years, every effort to bring moderate Southern Baptists into the ABC has failed. For some time, moderate Southern Baptists refused to accept the inevitability of the conservative takeover of their denomination. Moreover, when overtures were made, there were all kinds of fears, suspicions, and even conflicts of interest. Some of the problems involved misunderstandings and mistakes dating back to the civil rights struggle, while others were all about personalities. Regardless, precious time was lost. Now, time is running out.

As the Cooperative Baptist Fellowship becomes more entrenched as an organization, its leadership will be increasingly less likely to join the ABC. Also, as the ABC continues to diminish, it becomes a less attractive partner. The next two or three years are crucial. The stakes are very high. I pray that leaders with great vision will emerge to make the right things happen. Fast.

As I have outlined how a major realignment for Baptists could be carried out, I have certainly realized that realignments would not be as easy for other denominations. Nevertheless, they must consider reconstructing their constituencies so that like-minded churches can be united in common mission and ministry. Improving the ability of denominations to meet the demands that face them in the twenty-first century requires unity among churches. To that end, realignment must be both studied and implemented.

The ways in which Baptists handle possible realignment in order to create more homogeneous groupings of churches probably will not work for denominations that are more hierarchical and offer less autonomy to local congregations. Other ways must be found for these hierarchical churches to realign churches and persons into units with similar beliefs and commitments.

I do not know how mainline denominations are going to do it, but there is little doubt among those experts in the sociology of religion that the realignment of their churches is essential. Too much diversity within any denomination paralyzes its growth and development. And right now there is too much diversity in all of them!

Prescription 6

Rethinking Ordination

Questioning Ordination

There is little doubt that one of the bright spots in my own denomination as well as in other mainline denominations has been our ability and willingness to bring people of color into our churches. African American and Hispanic congregations have joined our denomination in significant numbers over the past few years. This influx of people of color has covered over the fact that the predominantly white churches that traditionally have made up the denomination's membership have been showing significant signs of decline.

These new additions to American Baptist Churches could be a source of spiritual revitalization and enthusiasm. They often bring a vitality and excitement to our worship services that we desperately need. If they could become full participants in our denominational life, they could be a major force in turning our denomination around and setting us on a new path of dynamic ministry and growth. However, there are several things that are keeping this from happening. Of all of these hindering forces none are as significant as our ideas and practices related to ordination.

During the 1950s there was a concentrated effort on the part of the Ministers Council of the American Baptist Convention to make the clergy more "professional." This effort received a great deal of backing from the Ministers and Missionaries Benefit Board of the American Baptist Convention as this latter group sought guidelines to figure out who was and who was not eligible for their medical and retirement benefits. It was not long before a variety of resolutions at national and state level meetings established high and carefully delineated educational requirements for any who sought ordination as American Baptist clergy. College training followed by a seminary education was determined to be essential, and those without the proper academic qualifications were assigned second-class clergy status.

I do not think that denominational leaders have even begun to measure the effects of this decision. Most of our churches have fewer than a hundred members, and most have such limited financial support that they find themselves unable to pay the salary required to underwrite pastors who have this kind of education. After all, it takes several years and approximately $90,000 to get the education that qualifies a candidate for ordination.

Hispanics and African Americans, who often come from poverty, find such a financial burden too heavy to carry. Even more important, most of them are also trying to support their families with another job while they pastor. To tell them they also have to add going to seminary to their overloaded schedule is to ask more of them than we should.

Among the eighty-three pastors who make up the Hispanic Clergy of Philadelphia, eighty of them have to be bivocational in order to make a decent living. None of these eighty pastors would qualify for full ordination in my denomination or in any other mainline church.

My own denomination, like several others, tries to compensate those pastors who cannot meet its educational requirement for ordination by offering them licenses to be lay ministers. But this just will not suffice. We are saying to them in no uncertain terms that they are not as qualified to serve their churches as seminary graduates would be. To that, they are likely to ask: In what *ways* are seminary graduates better

qualified than we are to pastor our churches? Have they
learned what goes on in the governmental housing projects
and on the streets? Do they understand the violence that has
become commonplace in urban neighborhoods? Do they understand the workings of the police and the power politics of
cities? Do these graduates of yours have any sense of the
nihilism that has gripped urban youth? Do they have even a
semblance of knowledge about what it means to be poor?
Don't the life experiences of those who minister in "the hood"
year after year count for anything?

No wonder so many of our Hispanic and African American
pastors have antidenominational biases. Since they are rejected for full ordination in mainline denominations, is it
surprising that they reject the groups that have rejected
them?

We cannot afford to alienate these pastors and their
churches. We need the vitality that they can bring to the rest
of us. We need their support and participation if we are to
reach the exploding populations among Hispanics and African Americans. And these struggling churches need us too.
They need our financial support as well as the human resources we can bring to their efforts. Denominational affiliation can help them into stability and strength as well as give
them a strong sense of being part of the larger body of Christ.
But they will not be part of our fellowship if their pastors are
labeled as second-class citizens because we refuse them
first-class ordination.

I am tired of hearing denominational officials tell me that
they cannot get people of color to participate in their conventions and other activities. Well, what we are saying with our
ordination requirements is not only an alienating judgment
on their pastors but also on them.

The whole system seems non-Baptist to me. I have to ask
if we American Baptists really do believe in the autonomy
of the local church. If we do, shouldn't we be ready to
concede that it is up to the members of the local congregation
to determine what qualifications are needed in someone

they would call to shepherd them?

Personally, I think the whole system reeks of academic elitism. We seem to be reluctant to believe that Scripture is speaking to the church in the present age when it tells us:

> Because the foolishness of God is wiser than men; and the weakness of God is stronger than men. For ye see your calling, brethren, how that not many wise men after the flesh, not many mighty, not many noble, are called: But God hath chosen the foolish things of the world to confound the wise; and God hath chosen the weak things of the world to confound the things which are mighty; And base things of the world, and things which are despised, hath God chosen, yea, and things which are not, to bring to nought things that are (1 Corinthians 1:25-28).

I think it's time to ask ourselves whether or not we believe what the Bible itself tells us about who is capable of inter-preting and preaching its message. I argue that we have become worshipers of academia and that we have more confidence in how a background in theology and biblical languages prepares preachers to interpret Scripture than we have in the work of the Holy Spirit. I believe that truth from God does not come from the top down, but rather, from the bottom up. I believe that God chooses to reveal messages to us not through an elite group of specialists, but rather through the body of Christ. While I appreciate hermeneutical scholarship, I do not believe that God's truth is primarily discerned through an academic process. I believe that God's truth becomes known through the collective understanding of seemingly ordinary people who bind themselves together in a common commitment to Christ's lordship.

Learning through Liberation Theology

To illustrate what I am trying to say, let me take you back several decades to a time when the pope, concerned about the Protestant inroads being made in Latin America, called upon North American Catholics to send missionaries there to renew and rebuild the Roman Church. American Catholics, especially the Maryknoll brothers and sisters, responded to this call with enthusiasm. Soon thousands of Catholic missionaries were spreading out across the southern half of the Western Hemisphere with a commitment to call Latin American people back to the faith in which they were baptized.

But all of Latin America was not to be so easily reached. To do what the pope believed needed to be done would have required not thousands of missionary priests and nuns, but hundreds of thousands. Those that did go did the best they could, but the task was too vast for them. In response to the situation, some of them gradually came up with an idea that they believed would enable them to reach many more people using their same limited resources. It was the idea of creating "base communities."

These base communities were initially nothing more than Bible study groups established to help poor, uneducated people to carry on prayer and spiritual reflection by themselves. Like the old Methodist circuit riders on the American frontier of the nineteenth century, Catholic missionaries moved from village to village initiating these base communities. Soon there were thousands of them in place. But as was true of the Methodist circuit riders, these roving Catholic pastors could not visit their little flocks as often as they would have liked. Weeks, and sometimes months, passed before return visits could be made, and in the absence of the ordained clergy, the poor and simple peasants of base communities were left to study the Bible on their own.

Equipped with no helps other than the Holy Spirit, people in these base communities prayerfully worked on the Scriptures and tried to figure out how they applied to their own everyday lives. They were more successful in this venture than anyone would have imagined. When the "official" priests returned, they were often amazed at the brilliant insights that these peasants had gained without the benefit of their scholarship. It was out of these base communities that one of the most dynamic and controversial religious movements of our times emerged—liberation theology.

As the beaten-down peasants in rural villages and the slum dwellings of urban areas studied Scripture, they came up with some surprising interpretations of the biblical message. Unaided by erudite commentaries and "informed" scholars, these simple people leaned on each other for their understanding of what they were reading. The results were astounding.

Perhaps one of the most insightful discoveries that these Catholic Christians made was that God has a preferential commitment to the poor. Generally, in times past, the Scriptures had been used to legitimate the ruling establishment, even when those who held power were unjustly oppressive. The clergy usually supported those in power by citing Romans 13:1-2:

> Let every soul be subject unto the higher powers. For there is no power but of God: the powers that be are ordained of God. Whosoever therefore resisteth the power, resisteth the ordinance of God: and they that resist shall receive to themselves damnation.

These verses were interpreted to mean that civil disobedience was not an option for Christians. Rebellion against those who held political power was interpreted, according to this passage, to be rebellion against God.

In the class struggle between the rich and powerful on the one hand and the poor and the oppressed on the other, God was defined as having taken sides with the former against the latter. But all of that changed when the Scriptures were read through the eyes of those who were the socially and economically disinherited. What came out for the base communities was a new image of God. Those who huddled together around lanterns in their shacks and huts discovered in Scripture a God who, in the struggles between the rich and poor, had sided with the poor. They found that from the beginning of time, God was at work in the world championing the cause of the powerless and downtrodden.

Their new scriptural insights led them to realize that out of all the peoples of the earth, God chose as His elect a people in Egypt who were downtrodden and enslaved. As these people cried out in their despair, God heard their cry and declared that He would fight for them against their oppressors.

Later, when the children of Israel had established themselves in the Promised Land, the God of the Bible again stood up for the poor and the wretched. As in any societal system, a class structure emerged in Israel. There were upper-class Jews who had the power and the wealth, and there were lower-class Jews who bore the brunt of their tyranny. But as the poor in the base communities read the Bible, they were surprised to learn that God sided with the poor and sent prophets to demand justice and compassion for them. Biblical giants like Amos and Isaiah were discovered to be spokesmen for *them*, and to espouse *their* cause.

> Ye that lie upon beds of ivory, and stretch themselves upon their couches, and eat the lambs out of the flock, and the calves out of the midst of the stall. Therefore now shall they go captive with the first that go captive, and the banquet of them that stretched themselves shall be removed (Amos 6:4,7).

> Woe unto them that decree unrighteous decrees, and that write grievousness which they have prescribed. To turn aside the needy from judgment, and to take away the right from the poor of my people, that widows may be their prey, and that they may rob the fatherless! And what will ye do in the day of visitation, and in the desolation which shall come from far? to whom will ye flee for help? and where will ye leave your glory? Without me they shall bow down under the prisoners, and they shall fall under the slain. For all this his anger is not turned away, but his hand is stretched out still (Isaiah 10:1-4).

Too often liberation theology is viewed as being the creation of some neo-Marxist intellectuals who simply use the Bible to recast their own Communist doctrine. While those like José Bonino, Gustavo Gutiérrez, and James Luis Segundo (who have written tomes on liberation theology) get all the press, they are not the source of it. It is a theology that comes from the people. It is a way of reading the Bible that frees it from the blinders that the powerful elite have put on the church for far too many years.

When the Catholic missionaries returned and listened to the interpretations of Scripture developed by these uneducated and hardly literate people in the base communities, they were humbled. These educated clerics soon realized that something supernational was going on and that these small groups meeting in the name of Jesus had received truth from beyond themselves. God had given to these simple people an understanding of Scripture that made their sophisticated hermeneutics seem like foolishness by comparison.

The depth of the insights of these common peasants, the relevance of their explanations of the meaning of Scripture to the affairs of their lives, and the growing spirituality that seemed increasingly evident among them taught the missionaries that they themselves were there to learn from these people. These missionaries who had come from the north to minister to the peasants sensed that God was instead ministering to them through these humble people who had become sacramental agents. The clergy had to learn anew that the Holy Spirit is the ultimate teacher and that the Spirit reveals truth through those whom the world calls simple and inferior.

My reason for digressing into this description of the evolution of liberation theology is to make the claim that these Catholics have discovered a truth that lies at the heart of what it means to be Baptist. They have discovered the basis on which we establish authority for the local church.

Many of us are convinced that something mystical happens when people join together to seek the will of Christ and to experience him in a shared manner. There can be, we say, a collective encounter with Christ that transcends anything that the members of such a group can know individually.

There is a reality, a revolutionary power, and a sense of shared ecstasy that sets the group apart from what can be experienced on an individual level.

Bringing Things Back Home

The Bible makes it clear that such a collective experience with Christ gave birth to the Christian church. We read about this in Acts 2:1-4:

> And when the day of Pentecost was fully come, they were all with one accord in one place. And suddenly there came a sound from heaven as of a rushing mighty wind, and it filled all the house where they were sitting. And there appeared unto them cloven tongues like as of fire, and it sat upon each of them. And they were all filled with the Holy Ghost, and began to speak with other tongues, as the Spirit gave them utterance.

The amazing events of the day of Pentecost have been repeated over and over again in the life of the church. There have been regular outpourings of the Holy Spirit on people who get together to seek God's presence and leading. Jesus promised that this would happen when he said to his disciples: "And let us consider one another to provoke unto love and to good works: Not forsaking the assembling of ourselves together, as the manner of some is; but exhorting one another: and so much the more, as ye see the day approaching" (Hebrews 10:24-25).

What I am trying to say in all of this is that a local congregation possesses in such a shared consciousness sufficient authority to discern God's will. Truth emerges from the bottom up, rather than from the top down. Authority does not flow from those who speak from positions at the top of denominational hierarchies. When it comes to ordination of candidates for the ministry, there is no need to go to higher levels of a religious bureaucracy to secure approval for who should lead a local congregation.

The regional associations and national organizations are

useful for helping local churches to carry out such ministries as foreign missionary work and educational programs that they would not be able to accomplish individually. But when these larger organizational bodies take it upon themselves to determine who ought to be pastoring a local congregation, I think that they have gone beyond their prerogatives. Authority for such decisions should flow out of the mystical togetherness of assembled Christians of a local congregation.

This base community model for studying Scripture raises some very serious questions as to who is "ordained" to interpret Scripture. Is it the academically qualified seminary graduate who is the conduit of revelation, or is the truth revealed through a body of committed believers who together seek the leading of their Lord? Is it the educated expert in biblical studies or the local body of Christ that holds the truth in earthen vessels? I am arguing here against an emphasis on clerical authority that reeks of professionalism, and I am questioning the claim that the educational credentials prescribed by denominational bodies should be a requisite for ordination. In case you haven't figured it out, I believe the local church has the spiritual authority to determine who should or shouldn't be ordained for its ministry.

Is the Concept of Ordination Unbiblical?

I make my argument in the context of some theological reflection that was encouraged as part of my denomination's programming. In 1964 American Baptists joined with other Baptist groups from around the world and declared the Baptist Jubilee Advance. This was to be a special year of Baptist evangelism and mission. As part of preparing for that special evangelistic thrust, American Baptists were urged to read the book by Markus Barth entitled *The Broken Wall*. This book was a commentary on Paul's Epistle to the Ephesians.

Among the many truths this book made clear was that *every* Christian was called to be a minister of the gospel. Ministry, Barth made clear, was not the prerogative of a special elite. The local body of Christ is made up of many members and all of them are ordained for ministry. Some have special gifts such as preaching and teaching, but it is not just these gifted people who are to be ordained to ministry. All in the body are ordained for ministry, and these gifted persons are given the task of building up the rest of those who are in the body so that they might minister more effectively to the world. Barth made clear that this was a proper interpretation of Ephesians 4:11-12: "And he gave some, apostles; and some, prophets; and some, evangelists; and some, pastors and teachers; For the perfecting of the saints, for the work of the ministry, for the edifying of the body of Christ."

There is a place for biblical scholarship, homiletical expertise, theological education, and pastoral care. But those who carry out such ministries, according to this passage, do not have to have some special kind of ordination that puts them in some special category of holiness. Instead, these specially gifted persons are to build up all the rest of the members of the church, all of whom are ordained.

What is even more significant is that Paul actually diminishes the importance of those who have the gifts that make them the "up-front" people in the church. Those who stand behind the pulpit and preach are important and those who teach from the lectern are significant, but Paul makes it clear that those who often go unnoticed are usually the more essential members for the ongoing work of the church: "Nay, much more those members of the body, which seem to be more feeble, are necessary: And those members of the body, which we think to be less honourable, upon these we bestow more abundant honour; and our uncomely parts have more abundant comeliness" (1 Corinthians 12:22-23).

The validity of Paul's teaching was brought home to me one Saturday evening when I was asked to preach at a country church in southern Indiana. I arrived more than an hour and a half before the service was scheduled to start, and the only person around was an old gentleman who seemed to be checking things out. He was making sure that there were hymnals in every pew, that the thermostat was properly set, and that the church bulletins were neatly placed on the table in the church vestibule. As we met, I introduced myself and then asked him if he was the pastor of the church. He laughed and said no. I followed up with asking him if he might be the custodian, and again I got a chuckle and a no. The old gentleman then said, "What you have here is an old codger that God has given the gift of helps."

"Check it out," he said, "the twelfth chapter of First Corinthians, verse 28, talks about that gift. I am ordained to the ministry of helps. We get young preachers to serve this little church. They come and go and sometimes we can't even remember their names. They're all important, I suppose. But one of these days, I'm going to die, and then they'll realize just how important I am. The next Sunday the hymnbooks won't be in place and the heat won't be turned up. And if it snows, nobody will shovel the sidewalk. Then they'll know how important it is to have somebody around who's ordained to the ministry of helps."

Given the fact that each of us is ordained for ministry just like that old man, I have to ask what right any denominational hierarchy has to contend that there are those who fail to qualify because of the lack of academic degrees.

I know that what I am suggesting is radical, but we're living in a time when radical thinking is needed. Maybe the time has come to get rid of the whole idea of ordination and, in so doing, open up the church to a whole new way of thinking about ministry.

I do not find in the Bible the kind of ordination that has come to typify mainline denominations. Respecting the belief that traditions arise in Christendom under the leadership of the Holy Spirit, I accept the idea of ordaining the clergy. But when the clergy becomes "professionalized" with academic qualifications and other "essentials," I have to raise my voice in objection. I believe that it is the prerogative of the local church to determine who should be ordained. Furthermore,

I contend that the larger denominational fellowship should have the right to decide only which churches should be full-fledged members. Whichever churches prove acceptable for denominational membership should be able to claim that those whom they have chosen and ordained on the local level be accepted as ordained by the larger fellowship of churches. A denomination should be able to recommend that academic and other qualifications be possessed by such pastors. But that is all it should do. It should only recommend. I claim radical autonomy and authority for the local congregation.

I am sure that you can figure out how my suggestion could be a boon for Hispanic and African American churches. But there would also be dramatic benefits for the denomination itself if the autonomy of the local church could be radically established as part of the polity of not only my own denomination, but for other mainline churches as well. The advantages for mainline denominations is what the next chapter is all about.

Prescription 7

Asserting the Autonomy of the Local Church

In the American Baptist denomination, each church is a law unto itself. Unlike Presbyterians, Methodists, or Episcopalians, the local congregation of believers owns its church property. The number of denominational programs suggested by the national leadership that are implemented by any given congregation is completely determined by the members of that congregation.

This, of course, has been a source of endless frustration for denominational executives over the years. It is a fact that when denominational leaders had some programs for evangelism or social action to promote, there was no way they could *make* any local congregations participate. If they had some new church school curriculum to introduce or some requisite for the organization or function of local congregations, all that could be done was to *suggest*. It was up to the local congregations to make the final decisions as to the extent that cooperation would be forthcoming, if at all.

Perhaps most disturbing for those in positions of national leadership has been their inability to access from local congregations monies needed to run their denomination's programs and missionary work. For American Baptist Churches, the amount the local church contributed to the annual budget has been totally a matter of local church discretion.

But now the doctrine of autonomy, which has been the bane of their existence, could possibly be a blessing in disguise for denominational leaders. This doctrine could prove to be the salvation of a denomination facing the possibility of a destructive split. If each church could decide for itself what is right or wrong, the handling of such explosive issues as abortion or homosexuality could be sent back to local congregations. Each local congregation could be called upon to determine what policies it should establish on such matters. Each could do so with the understanding that its decisions would be unchallenged by those at the national headquarters of the denomination and could not be overruled by a vote on some resolution at the annual convention of church representatives. Decisions made by any one congregation would be binding only upon that congregation. Thus, one American Baptist congregation could go on record as being pro-life while a neighboring church might be identified as being pro-choice. One church might take a strong stand against behavior that involves same-gender genital contact while another could establish itself as a "welcoming and affirming congregation."

The arguments generated by the culture wars discussed earlier cannot be settled by clever diplomacy. Any denominational executive who thinks that it is possible to get the combatting sides to simply smile and agree to disagree is doing a lot of wishful thinking. The differences that separate the sides do not lend themselves to compromise because what is at stake is the very essence of what each side believes is at the core of what it means to be Christian.

Those on the evangelical side contend that what is at stake is more than just issues over sexuality; it is the authority of the Bible. To give in, they believe, is to give up on their belief that the Bible pronounces truth in ultimate and final fashion. One intense evangelical asked me, "If the Bible doesn't speak with absolute authority on homosexuality or abortion, then how do I know whether or not it is speaking with absolute authority when it speaks on salvation?"

Those who would call themselves moderates or progressives are equally adamant because they view the mission of the church to be the declaration of the liberating presence of Christ in the world. They believe that the gospel is the good news that Christ is at work in the world freeing his people from the oppression and dehumanization that have been laid on them by a demonically controlled society. The denigrating of homosexuals (often at the hands of the church) and the oppression of women (as seen in denying them the right to determine their own biological destinies) are prime examples to them of what Christ came to abolish.

To believe that two such divergent perspectives on the essence of Christianity can be reconciled with simple declarations that God has called us to love and accept one another in spite of our differences is extremely naive. However, there is a way of handling the conflicts generated by the culture wars so that people in the pews do not feel that their consciences are being violated as they maintain affiliation with a denomination that includes churches that hold convictions different from their own. High on the list of what must be done to work things out is to *assert the autonomy of the local church*. One reason that the American Baptist Churches is such a good case study for us is because the denomination already has a commitment to this belief and practice.

It is not difficult to figure out that such an arrangement could create a certain amount of confusion. Diversity always creates *some* confusion. Theologies, practices, programs, and styles of worship would be established by each local congregation, and you would never know what you were getting into when you walked into an American Baptist church; each church would be somewhat unique in beliefs and practices. In reality, that is what you would find right now. The variations that exist from one American Baptist church to another are often so great that it is only after you have a chance to survey the church program, ask some pertinent questions, review what goes on during worship, and have a general understanding of its people that you really can get a handle on what the church is all about. Quite simply, asserting autonomy for the local church would not create any more diversity among American Baptists than already exists.

To carry this suggestion to a logical limit, I suggest that even ordination become the prerogative of each local church. I believe that each separate congregation should be given the right and the power to decide for itself whether or not to grant endorsement to any particular man or woman that it chooses. That way a homosexual person could be endorsed by a given church that deemed him or her worthy and qualified for the pastoral ministry while another congregation might not recognize the validity of that person's ordination. Ordination could be given without requiring any dissenting congregation in the denomination to go against its conscience by being expected to recognize or approve of homosexual practices. On the other hand, a "welcoming and affirming" congregation would not feel compromised if another American Baptist church ordained to the gospel ministry someone who did not approve of persons in that particular homosexual lifestyle.

Some will throw up their hands in horror and say that what I am suggesting would lead to denominational anarchy. Perhaps so. But we have to find some way for churches with divergent convictions to live together and work together. In spite of their differences, there are ways our churches can work together on many important ministries in which we have a common interest. I fully realize that what I am suggesting here is a whole new view of what a denomination is, how it is structured, and how it functions.

Of course, things are never this simple. Questions would still be raised about what standards for faith and practice would be established for those who hold offices and serve in executive positions on the national denominational level. There would be questions about qualifications for serving as missionaries for such a diverse denomination. But I am convinced that even these problems could be solved through careful planning and negotiations, and I want to make sug-

careful planning and negotiations, and I want to make suggestions for such solutions.

The time has come to recognize that the tendencies toward decentralization and localism are prevalent in the culture. Hierarchical systems of control are being challenged everywhere. In politics, both Democrats and Republicans are vying to make government smaller. Both parties are offering to give back decision-making power to local communities so that people can come up with solutions to their own problems. There is a growing consensus that those who are removed from where the action is have no real comprehension of what is going on or how to address the existential situations. Increasingly, there is a call to let people come together on the local level so that they can make the decisions that determine their own destinies.

We are seeing the emergence of localism in Christian ministries and mission work as well. Habitat for Humanity brilliantly models the localization of beliefs and practices within a huge international ministry. This year Habitat will build well over ten thousand homes around the world. Its leader, Millard Fuller, has been a driving force in inspiring groups of people to come together on the local level and form affiliates, each of which is committed to building houses in its own neighborhood.

In its early years, the Habitat organization had much discussion about how Christianity would be expressed in its ministry. There was never any doubt that Habitat would be known as a Christian ministry enterprise and that its primary base of support would be among church people. But there were questions as to how theologically doctrinaire Habitat would be:

Would Jewish people be allowed to participate in the same ways as Christians?

While homeowners are each given a Bible as part of the dedication of their new homes, how much should Habitat endeavor to evangelize these people into a personal relationship with Christ?

To what extent would Habitat define itself as a Christian ministry in evangelical terms?

What finally emerged was a consensus to leave it up to local affiliates to answer such questions.

As a member of the advisory board of Habitat, I am often asked if Habitat is an evangelical organization. I always respond that each local affiliate answers that question in its own way. I know of local Habitat affiliates that make witnessing with the Four Spiritual Laws of Campus Crusade a part of their ministry. And I know of other affiliates where the name of Jesus is rarely mentioned. In each case, people in the local affiliates determine the religious character of their mission. In answer to the question of how theologically liberal or conservative Habitat is, I can only say, "It's whatever you in the local affiliate decide it should be."

Fuller himself contends that he believes in the "theology of the hammer" (the title of one of his books). He has found that when people come together and build a house, they discover a great sense of spiritual oneness that transcends their individual differences. In working together, people realize that they are brothers and sisters in Christ in spite of their wide diversity of opinions on some of the crucial issues of our time. Fuller argues that the kind of discussions that take place as people come alongside each other while hammering nails allows for a coming together that would never take place in the heated discussions of a denominational conclave.

Localism works for Habitat for Humanity, and I believe it could work in denominational ministries as well. There are many things that people with divergent theological beliefs could do together that would foster understanding and commonalities of commitment to service without compromising basic convictions. It would take a great deal of creative thinking to figure out how to make such a plan functional for denominational ministries, but it can be done.

There is a further consideration that we should make as we think about the shift to localism that seems everywhere

evident across America—that is, whether or not denominational programs really make any sense at all on the local
level. Is it really sensible to design programs at some national
denominational office and expect them to be relevant to what
goes on in the communities where churches establish their
neighborhood ministries?

I am convinced that in the future, local churches will
develop their programs more in conjunction with other
churches in their own vicinity than by accepting what might
be prescribed for them from national denominational offices.
That is one reason why I see such positive possibilities for
mainline churches in the years that lie ahead. Mainline
churches have had a growing tradition for cooperation in
ministry. Unlike nondenominational evangelical churches
that often chart extremely independent courses for themselves, mainline churches expect to work together in address-
ing both the spiritual and social needs of the people who live
in their communities. There are communities in which mainline churches have already come together to design and
implement effective programs for people with AIDS, for the
homeless, for unwed mothers, and for youth. Cooperative
efforts have also been made through such efforts as CROP
walks to raise funds to meet the needs of the hungry in other
places in the world.

Doesn't it really make more sense for clergy and laity from
various mainline churches to come together and figure out
what needs to be done in the community and how best to do
it? Isn't it reasonable to assume that churches of different
denominations (but with a great deal in common so far as
theology and practice are concerned) can unify for the work
in the neighborhood that the church should be doing? Aren't
evangelistic outreach programs more readily acceptable to
folks when they are viewed as transcending denominational
labels?

Assuming that the answers to these questions are all "yes,"
it seems to me that maybe one thing for denominational
leaders to consider at this time in American life is to wind

down their emphasis on denominational programming and encourage localism. The motto of our times is "to think globally and act locally." That's something that the leaders of mainline churches should encourage. Such an approach would not only work better, but also would save denominations a lot of money. The time has come for radical localism in our thinking and acting as Christians.

Restructuring Missions

Economic considerations weigh heavily in the hard times mainline denominations are going through these days. Each denomination has to figure out how to get members in the local churches to send more dollars to their respective national headquarters. If the money does not come in, the ministries these denominations sponsor suffer.

But this is where problems related to the culture wars play themselves out with far-reaching effects. If a denomination endorses and supports programs that members in given local congregations find offensive, there is talk by that church of withholding funds from the denomination's coffers, and even of withdrawing the local congregation from denominational membership. Such threats have to be taken seriously by denominational executives because, in most instances, their programs are already underfunded. The declining membership of most denominations along with a decline in the spending capabilities of middle-class Americans has meant that there is less and less money available for the various ministries and missionary enterprises of mainline churches. In almost every case, these denominations have little in the way of financial reserves to carry them through any extended period of diminished income. What makes these financial pressures particularly hurtful is that it takes all available money just to keep existing programs going, and this is at a

time when there is a need to make significant investments
in new ministries such as youth work in the cities and relief
programs to the needy in Third World countries. There is a
great frustration among denominational officials who lack
the resources to develop the kind of programs that would
revitalize the ministries of their churches. When somebody
like me comes along and starts pointing out a host of things
that should be done if mainline denominations are to survive
into the twenty-first century, I can almost see them throw up
their hands in disgust and hear them mumble, "We don't need
some sociologist like you coming along to tell us what to do.
We need some dollars to do it!"

It is here that denominational executives might take a
page out of the methodology books of such parachurch organizations as Youth for Christ, Young Life, Campus Crusade,
Wycliffe Bible Translators, and Youth With A Mission
(YWAM), because each of these organizations has solved this
problem. Each of them has figured out how to raise the
millions of dollars needed to place tens of thousands of
missionaries on the field and also raise sufficient funds to
meet the needs of their home offices. Parachurch organizations have been able to be more innovative in their ministries
than mainline churches because they have had the financial
resources to try out everything from using television programming for evangelism to developing multimillion-dollar
relief and development agencies for helping Third World
countries.

For parachurch organizations, the primary means for raising money for programs has been to personalize fund-raising.
For instance, each candidate in a parachurch missionary
organization is required to raise his or her own personal
support. Only when sufficient funds have been pledged and
enough money is already in place to cover the expenses for
the first year of service, is the missionary candidate sent out
to the field. These candidates do deputation work in which
they make appeals to friends, relatives, and the members of
their home churches.

People are more willing to give to persons they know than to some seemingly impersonal, denominational, bureaucratically controlled missionary project. They have grown suspicious of large organizations and want to know exactly who is getting the money they give. By personalizing giving and asking people to pledge to specific missionary candidates, parachurch organizations allay such suspicions. When donors give to specific persons they have known for years, they are confident that they know what their missionaries will do on the field; when they give to denominational causes, they often have serious questions about who and what is being supported. In the current money-raising methods of mainline denominations, there is just too much social distance between the givers and the ministries being funded.

An incredibly effective missionary organization is Youth With A Mission. In spite of the fact that YWAM is just a few decades old, it has been able to deploy more than forty thousand field workers. This has been possible only because the organization requires each missionary candidate to raise his or her own financial support. Wycliffe Bible Translators, in like manner, has been able to place more than thirty-six thousand missionaries on the field.

These figures of YWAM and Wycliffe are even more dramatic when compared with the 250 missionaries presently supported by my own old and historic denomination of 1.5 million members. What must be increasingly disheartening for those in charge of mission work for mainline denominations such as the American Baptist Churches is the discovery that people in their churches are more and more giving to such parachurch organizations and missionary programs. The personal associations that the members of mainline churches have with these missionary candidates who make direct appeals for help elicit more loyalty and support from them than could ever be gained from what usually appears to be religious bureaucracies. Thus, it is not surprising that independent missionaries and parachurch organizations are siphoning off a huge portion of the missionary giving that might otherwise be available for ministries of mainline churches.

I believe that it is time for mainline denominations to begin utilizing this same style of fund-raising. I am proposing that missionaries and those who lead specialized ministries in these mainline churches individually raise their own financial support.

Even as I make this suggestion, I can imagine the outcry of those who are in charge of denominational missionary programs, and even from the missionaries themselves. I can imagine them saying to one another, "This is just what we've been fighting against through the years, and now this sociologist is asking us to initiate a fund-raising system that we have come to detest."

Arguments for and Against

Arguments against this suggestion are easy to come by. First and foremost is the claim that those who will prove to be the most effective workers on the mission field may not necessarily be very effective at deputation work. Consequently, there would be a greater possibility that we might end up with good fund-raisers on the field instead of those with the spiritual gifts and the personal qualities most needed for service to indigenous people. People who talk a smooth line are not always the most desirable missionaries.

Second, deputation work takes a lot of time and detracts heavily from time spent in actual ministry. I know of one missionary couple who are away from the field raising money about one-third of their time. For every two years they are on the field, they are home for a year going around speaking to churches and meeting with people in order to shore up their base of financial support.

Does not this method of fund-raising prove wasteful? Does it not keep missionaries worrying about support rather than concentrating on their work?

While these are good and powerful reasons for being opposed to my suggestion, I have some other reasons, besides its effectiveness for bringing in money, to recommend this plan for mainline denominations. First and foremost is the fact that it establishes a network of people to pray for missionaries. Those who raise financial support by personally recruiting donors not only establish a number of people who regularly donate money, they also establish a network of people who are most likely to undergird them in prayer. Jesus said: "Where your treasure is, there will your heart be also." The relationship of this truth to missionary work is obvious. People pray for those individuals to whom they give their missionary dollars.

Whenever we consider the ministries of the church, we are apt to say that we should pray for those who lead them. In reality, however, these servants of the kingdom and the work that they do seldom come to mind. But all of that changes when we become financially involved with their ministries in a directly personal manner.

Those who make monthly contributions to support a particular missionary are likely to have a photo of that missionary tacked to a bulletin board or on display near a work desk to serve as a prayer reminder. When checks are written, prayers are prayed. Financial involvement often carries with it spiritual commitment. And I believe that the prayers that regularly go up from that network of those who financially support a particular missionary are more important than the financial gifts themselves. I am not just saying that—I really believe it!

Second, having individual missionaries do deputation work to raise their own support will make it possible to get people to the field who otherwise would not get there. Over the years, I have recruited many young people for the cause of missions, most of whom have come from denominational churches. When these young people presented themselves as missionary candidates to the mission boards of their respective denominations, they often were turned down. It was not that they lacked the necessary qualifications or education. Neither was it a matter of their not being needed. Instead, their failure to gain placement for missionary service was due to the simple fact that their denominational programs lacked the financial means to place them.

Executives of the missionary organizations of mainline churches sometimes fail to face a very important fact. That is, that young people who are called to do mission work are not likely to give up that calling simply because their denominational programs have no openings for them. In all likelihood, these young people will turn to some independent mission board that is more than willing to bring them on board. I say more than willing because part of the individual support that such independent missionary candidates raise goes to support the administration of the independent mission board itself. Thus, the more missionaries recruited, the more money these independent mission boards will receive to invest in the development of their overall programs.

Back in the late 1960s, I was a speaker for an American Baptist conference for college and career young people. In the message that I delivered at that conference, I made a strong appeal to young people to give themselves to missionary service. A young woman responded to that call and offered herself to the cause. Unfortunately, when this young woman presented herself to the Board of International Ministries of our denomination, it was at the wrong time. They could not find a place for her in the American Baptist missionary program, in spite of her many gifts and her training as a nurse.

But this young woman was determined. Having heard the call, she was committed to living it out. She found out about an opportunity with the Sudan Interior Mission, an independent nondenominational missionary society. They accepted her, and soon she was hard at work raising the necessary support to go to Africa as a missionary.

Her home church, which was American Baptist, chipped in generously. To the members of her home church, it made little difference that she was getting linked up with a nondenominational missionary society. She was *theirs*! She had been the little girl in their primary department. She had been the teenager who was president of their youth fellowship group. She had been the soprano in the church choir.

The people in her home church gave what they could to make sure that she got to live out her missionary calling. If the ABC would not provide her with an opportunity for service, they would give to whatever group that would. They supported her with money that otherwise might have gone to the ABC programs, but that made little difference to them. To them, it was enough that they were supporting the cause of Christ as it was being presented by "their own little girl."

Stories like this could be told over and over again, thousands of times. It is surprising how many of those serving with parachurch missionary organizations come from American Baptist churches.

There is a third reason for adopting this fund-raising approach. It is that it would allay some of the concerns about mainline denominations that have grown up as a result of the culture wars. The individuals and churches that are intensely committed to ideological positions on such issues as abortion and homosexuality are so committed that they find it difficult to financially support a denomination that is not in harmony with their views. Those on either side of the divide in the culture wars demand that those who take denominational leadership roles share their beliefs on such issues. However, there is a way to overcome this seeming impasse. It is by allowing support to be designated exclusively to specific missionaries and specific programs.

What this would mean, of course, is that members of a denomination would be voting with their pocketbooks and encouraging those who have like-minded ideas. This certainly beats the present system wherein those with intense views often feel that they have been outmaneuvered by bureaucratic technicalities and parliamentary procedures every time resolutions on these issues are raised at conventions, conferences, synod meetings, and general assemblies. It could end the endless rounds of argument that go on at these gatherings as members demand to know whether or not their mission money is being used to support programs and missionaries that conflict with their particular convictions. It could be a major means for heading off a possible denominational schism.

Furthermore, what have denominational leaders got to lose? People without this option who are deeply committed on these issues will most likely give their missionary dollars only to those who support their beliefs and practices—even if those they support are outside their own denomination. Why not allow them to designate their giving to those who hold similar convictions within denominational ranks? It seems to me that this would be better than losing their support altogether. It just may be that the best ways to raise support for missionaries and denominational programs have changed, and those who lead mainline churches need to seriously reconsider their own methods.

Help from the Presbyterians

One mainline denomination that has seen the handwriting on the wall and has decided to explore some alternatives to their former fund-raising practices is the Presbyterian Church (USA). Right now the Presbyterians are exploring a proposal that allows for churches and individuals to have more control over where their mission money goes, while at the same time delivering missionaries from the intense fund-raising responsibilities that my earlier proposal would require. At a recent General Assembly meeting of the Presbyterian Church (USA), a resolution was introduced to restructure mission giving so that individual Presbyterians could support specific missionary projects. According to this proposal, a missionary would be appointed by a given presbytery to serve in a particular missionary project with which the presbytery had special ties; this arrangement would include a commitment for financial support. *(Note: Presbyteries are subdivisions of synods. They embrace the churches of a given region within*

a state; the organization that embraces all the presbyteries of a geographical region is called a synod.)
There is a strong likelihood that the churches of a given presbytery would tend to have similar beliefs and practices. It is a known fact, for instance, that the Presbytery of Philadelphia tends toward conservative politics and evangelical theology, while the Presbytery of Rochester, New York, has much more liberal tendencies. Consequently, candidates for the ministry tend to seek ordination in the context of presbyteries that express their own theological and socio-political leanings.

If this resolution becomes law in the Presbyterian Church (USA), then the same thing would happen to missionaries. They would be sent out by presbyteries rather than the denomination as a whole. Since local churches exercise more control over decision-making processes on the presbytery level, these churches would then be in a better position to determine which missionaries and mission projects they would fund.

Let us say that a given presbytery was highly evangelistic and the constituency of its churches was largely pro-life. The churches in that presbytery could ensure that the missionary hospital they supported in a Third World country would not perform abortions. They could also appoint missionaries who have strong commitments to traditional evangelicalism.

On the other hand, a liberal presbytery could follow a different course of action so far as medical practices were concerned and might even embrace a theology of missions that did not focus on winning persons to Christ.

This proposal does not offer perfect answers to all the problems. Of course, there would be particular churches and individual persons who would find such an arrangement oppressive so far as their own convictions are concerned. But overall, the enacting of this proposal would give people in local churches a much greater sense of having power to influence what is done in missionary work. It would deliver them from the sense that some bureaucrats at the faraway denominational headquarters are controlling what is going on without much regard for what the people in the pews want or think.

Sociologists, since the Lloyd Warner study of *Yankee City*, have known that discontent and rebellion are most likely to take place when people on the grass-roots level feel alienated from the decision-making processes and believe that they have little control over their destiny. Certainly grass-roots Presbyterians have been moved to discontent and near rebellion against their denominations for exactly these reasons. Adopting this resolution, which would shift the decision-making power for appointing missionaries and determining what kind of work they will do, would go a long way to quieting that discontent and diminishing the tendencies toward rebellion.

There is no reason why other denominations could not follow the Presbyterian model. In the United Methodist denomination, each district that makes up a conference could become a sponsoring missionary agency, supporting persons and projects that are in harmony with their specific beliefs and practices.

Certainly this model being explored by the Presbyterians has great possibilities for my own denomination, the American Baptist Churches. This national denomination is broken down into regions. Each region is, in turn, broken down into smaller units called associations. Consideration could be given to having each association sponsor particular missionaries and specific programs. That way local churches would be more likely to end up supporting missionaries and programs that reflect their particular beliefs and convictions.

Such a restructuring of missionary support systems could be the salvation of many mainline denominations that are precariously close to schism over faith and practice. As I have already pointed out, implementing such a proposal would not solve all our problems. The tensions resulting from the theological and culture wars that now threaten denominational unity do not lend themselves to simple solutions. This imperfect solution, however, may be worth a serious try.

One thing is certain: the time is gone when those in the national headquarters of mainline denominations can remain unchallenged as they designate who will serve as missionaries and what mission work will be done. The people in the pews will not put up with that any more. They want their missionary dollars going to ministries that represent their beliefs and commitments. If mainline denominations are going to survive into the twenty-first century, they had better figure out very soon how to make that happen.

Conclusion

Mainline denominations *can* be saved. The real question is, Why bother? If denominational labels no longer mean anything, if the culture wars have left hopelessly divided mainline churches trapped in outdated alliances, then why not simply dissolve those alliances altogether? If the local church is indeed the best and most biblical agent of Christianity for recruiting and supporting pastors and missionaries and for evangelism, social change, and theological reflection, then what is the point of national and international ecclesiastical structures? If parachurch organizations and Christian publishers produce better youth ministry resources, Sunday school curriculum, and inspirational literature, then why keep pouring money into inefficient, disconnected programming bureaucracies? When everything is said and done, are mainline denominations doomed as dinosaurs of another era, or is there still a vital role for them in building the kingdom of God?

My answer to the question posed in the title of this book is a resounding yes! Not only do I believe mainline denominations *can* be saved, I believe they *must* be saved. Why? Because if our mainline denominations die, then with them dies a great and glorious part of our spiritual heritage and foundation in the eternal, invisible church of Jesus Christ.

First and foremost, we must keep these historic denominations alive because they embody the great theological traditions to which our contemporary church must continually answer. Whenever individual preachers or congregations lose touch with the Christian community and ignore the larger movement of God throughout history, they become vulnerable and even dangerous. The doctrines and practices they establish in their particular social contexts can all too easily become distorted by concepts and personal agendas that have nothing to do with the gospel. Without the checks and balances provided by Christian theological tradition, such pastors and congregations to some degree become *de facto* religious cults, examples of which are easy to find across America. When people presume to invent the Christian faith from scratch according to their own inclinations and prophecies, there is no end to the distorted interpretations of the Bible and the evil and anti-Christian practices they can produce.

In Matthew 13:52, Jesus taught that the kingdom of God was like a homeowner who opens his treasure chest to find something old and something new. While the church must always be changing to meet the challenges of a changing world, we must at the same time hold on to those enduring ideas and practices that continue to provide our substance and strength.

I remember the Jesus Movement, which sprang up on the West Coast during the 1960s, when thousands of young people dissatisfied with an amoral drug-addicted subculture turned to Pentecostal Christianity. Many of the churches and ministries that grew out of the Jesus Movement became wonderfully wholesome communicators of the faith, but some developed in strange and destructive ways. Among the worst of these was a cult called the Children of God, which became notorious for encouraging its female members to use sex to win potential converts.

A young woman I interviewed about the Children of God rhetorically asked, "After what Jesus did for me on the cross, why shouldn't I be willing to go to bed with a man for him?" She explained that the founder of her cult, Brother Mo, had received a new interpretation of the Bible that negated all that had come before and required women to sexually love people into the kingdom of God. It was terrible to see how easily this sincere believer had been led astray by a charismatic leader who had become a theological world unto himself.

Denominations are a safeguard against this sort of thing

because they require innovators to connect what is new to what is old, pulling heretical extremists back in line and testing their claims against Christian legitimacy.

In sociological terms, a strong and persistent collective consciousness exists in denominations. This collective consciousness is open to new ideas, but slow to fully incorporate them into the essential character and identity of the denomination, which means these new ideas must prove themselves over time. There is something mystical about this phenomenon, a sense in which denominational Christians recognize that they are part of an invisible church to which they must remain faithful. This is what the apostle Paul is referring to when he writes in Hebrews 12:1: "Wherefore seeing we also are compassed about with so great a cloud of witnesses, let us lay aside every weight, and the sin which doth so easily beset us, and let us run with patience the race that is set before us."

Another, related reason denominational Christianity must be saved is that it offers the best and safest alternatives for refugees from the culture wars who want to be part of a Christian community that is not subject to every wind of social change that blows across the American political landscape. The same stubborn resistance to change that in many ways threatens the survival of denominations is also, in this respect, a tremendous asset. In an increasingly fast-changing culture such as our own, the religious movements that reap short-term gains by keeping up with the trends risk long-term loss of spiritual credibility by forfeiting their identification with the eternal, unchanging, transcendent truth of God. In contrast, those denominations that remain steadfastly committed to their spiritual heritage and traditions emerge as the "classics," earning for themselves an aura of timelessness that corresponds to people's deepest religious wants and needs.

Right now, in the midst of an unprecedented surge in popularity, American evangelical Christianity is in many ways being co-opted by the Religious Right and the conser-

vative wing of the Republican party. Increasingly, many
evangelical leaders and churches are establishing for themselves a clearly political identity by strongly promoting a very
narrowly defined social agenda. Unfortunately, political
identities tend to quietly overshadow spiritual identities, and
I believe these leaders and churches will eventually find
themselves defined only in terms of their politics. Moreover,
in the years to come, many will discover the hard way that
such political identities are nearly impossible to erase.

The evangelical community will soon discover that Jesus
Christ is not a member of the Republican party, no matter
how convenient that might be at the moment. He is not a
Democrat either, of course, as some mainline denominational
leaders learned the hard way years ago. However, during the
sixties, when those leaders tried to make the Democratic
platform into denominational policy, there were enough opposing forces within their denominations to stop them. I see
no such balance in today's evangelical movement to guard
against reducing God's will for humanity to what is surely a
temporary partisan political movement.

Society is constantly reconstructed by fads and factions as
well as by great and lasting social changes, though at any
given time it may be hard to tell the difference. In such a
situation, it is easy for a particular church or leader to get
carried away by one issue or another. I do not mean only
politics, but also new trends and styles in morality, technology, music, and language, all of which invariably affect our
relationships with God and one another. That is why, in a
world where virtually everything seems to be changing, our
ongoing denominational traditions are so vitally important.
They keep us focused on and committed to those things that
truly matter and that do not change, even as everything
shakes loose around us, and they confirm that we are part of
a greater reality that transcends the ebb and flow of human
affairs.

In order to fulfill their purpose, however, mainline denominations must survive, and in order to survive they must

change. The proposals I have made in this book are not a blueprint as much as they are a call to action. I do not have all the answers, but I know we must find some soon. Each denomination will need great wisdom and discernment to figure out which is the baby and which is the bath water, to determine what should be strengthened and what should be discarded. All that is certain is that mainline denominations as they are presently organized cannot go on much longer.

In order to survive, denominations must recognize their true role as particular schools of thought within the larger Christian communities. This is one reason I favor the consolidation of denominational seminaries—in order to strengthen each denomination's sense of identity. It is vital that American Baptist pastors, evangelists, youth workers, and missionaries be trained in a way that is consistent with what is best about our spiritual heritage and tradition.

Indeed, it is hard to underestimate the importance of denominational seminaries if denominations themselves are understood as schools of thought. It is also hard to justify any longer the existence of programming bureaucracies. In order to serve their real purposes, a denomination's national programs and events must reflect that denomination's spiritual and theological distinctiveness. Therefore, in most cases, programs would be best planned at denominational colleges and seminaries by task forces of people actively engaged in ministry and theological reflection rather than by career executives in isolated national headquarters. College- and seminary-based task forces would also be better suited than denominational executives for the crucial task of creating or collaborating with Christian theologians to create church resources reflecting a denomination's particular school of thought. Such task forces would also be a lot less expensive, getting together only for specific, necessary jobs rather than requiring executives who hold ongoing positions.

Some denominations have already recognized the economy and benefits of locating their national headquarters on the campus of their educational institutions. Others, including the American Baptist Churches, should consider it now, even as they should consider the forms and functions of those seminaries themselves.

One thing we must recognize in all of this is that it is not just one denomination that must be saved and strengthened, but the network of relationships among the denominations whose cooperation and dialogue define and enrich the larger church of Jesus Christ. We Baptists need not only our spiritual heritage and traditions, but those of the United Methodists, the Lutherans, the Congregationalists, the Episcopalians, the Mennonites, and others. In some sense, we need the Roman Catholic church as well. Interdenominational cooperation and dialogue is and can be the setting for all kinds of spiritual growth as we are challenged and enriched by brothers and sisters in Christ who approach God very differently from the way we do.

Yes, denominations are important. Yes, they can be saved. And yes, saving them will require great and sometimes very painful changes. In considering this reconstruction, I have often been reminded of what Karl Barth said when plans were being made to rebuild the Pennsylvania train station at Madison Square Garden. "Tearing down the old station is not difficult," he remarked, "nor is building the new one. What is difficult is tearing down the old station and building the new one while keeping the trains running on time."

Every proposal I have made involves ongoing ministries and the real, live people who comprise them and who depend upon them in many ways. In reconstructing the American Baptist Churches or any other denomination for the twenty-first century, we must be very careful of these people. Even in cases that are clear-cut, we must be gentle as well as wise. If figuring out what to keep and what to discard is difficult, carrying out the process in a loving manner might seem virtually impossible, which brings me to my final conclusion.

Ultimately, the greatest necessity for the comeback of mainline denominations is not sociological analysis or theological reflection or even bold strategic planning. The greatest necessity is *spiritual revival*.

Throughout history, in particular times and places, the Holy Spirit has moved in powerful and miraculous ways to revive the church. People have come under conviction, repented of their sins, and experienced the reality of God in ways that literally transformed their lives. Sometimes these revivals transformed communities and even nations, but another result has always been growing churches, as spirit-filled believers come together for praise and worship, teaching, and fellowship.

Many of us who love God are praying for a revival in our place and in our time. We long to see America submit to God, accept Jesus Christ as Savior, and be filled with the Holy Spirit. We long to see an outpouring of grace transform our sin-sick society into part of God's great kingdom. Certainly we think and plan and work in the very best way we can, but in the end we know that the only real hope for the revival of our churches, the redemption of our communities, and the regeneration of our world is God.

We cannot make the Spirit do our bidding, for as Jesus tells us, "The wind [spirit] bloweth where it listeth, and thou hearest the sound thereof, but canst not tell whence it cometh, and whither it goeth: so is every one that is born of the Spirit" (John 3:8).

What we can do is pray.

Come quickly, Lord! Your church is weak and in disarray and only you can make it new again! Only you can make us, individually and corporately, what you want us to be! Only you can save us!

That great day will come, of course, but until then, we must keep on keeping on. We must not grow weary of trying to do what God would have us do to make our churches strong and effective agents of His ministry to the world. We must not give up trying to remake our denominations to better serve those churches. We must be faithful, whatever the cost, and be thankful that we have a part in building the kingdom of God.

Notes

Part I

Chapter 1

1. The American Baptist Convention changed its name to American Baptist Churches in the U.S.A. in 1972.
2. From "'Are Ye Able,' Said the Master"; words by Earl Marlatt.

Chapter 4

1. "Blest Be the Tie That Binds"; words by John Fawcett.
2. Words by James Russell Lowell.

Chapter 6

1. The Promise Keepers is an evangelical men's movement sponsoring massive gatherings that focus on traditional family values.
2. For an extended discussion of the debate over who can rightfully claim the name "evangelical," see the March/April 1995 issue of *Sojourners* magazine, which includes articles on the topic by Jim Wallis and myself. Copies are available from *Sojourners*, 2401 15th Street, NW, Washington, D.C., 20009. Phone: 202/328-8842.

Part II

Prescription 2

1. American Baptists are also related to the Evangelical Seminary of Puerto Rico, Morehouse School of Religion and the School of Theology of Virginia Union University. I have not included these schools in the discussion because each has a unique ministry to a specific ethnic group that a general seminary could not meet.